On Target English

Teacher's Resource Book

Year 2

Hilary Frost

PEARSON EDUCATION LIMITED
Edinburgh Gate, Harlow, Essex, CM20 2JE, England
and Associated Companies throughout the World.

First published 2001
Second impression 2002
© Hilary Frost 2001

The right of Hilary Frost to be identified as the author of this
Work have been asserted by her in accordance with the
Copyright, Designs and Patents Act of 1988.

All rights reserved. No part of this publication
may be reproduced, stored in a retrieval system,
or transmitted in any form or by any means, electronic,
mechanical, photocopying, recording, or otherwise,
without the prior written permission of the
Publishers or a licence permitting restricted copying in
the United Kingdom issued by the Copyright Licensing
Agency Ltd, 90 Tottenham Court Road, London,
W1P 9HE.

Printed in China
NPCC/02

ISBN 0 582 40914 4

Acknowledgements
The handwriting characters in this book were created using
Handwriting for Windows 2.0. This product enables the user to
create model handwriting in the size, colour and style of their
choice (including a dotted script). HfW2 runs on Windows 95
and above and is available from KBER (Kath Balcombe
Educational Resources). Please contact Customer Services for
details on 01743 356764.

The publisher's policy is to use paper manufactured from
sustainable forests.

Longman

Edinburgh Gate
Harlow,   Essex

Contents

Introduction 3

Key Concept Reference Charts
   Writing 6
   Grammar 7
   Sentence Construction and Punctuation 8
   Spelling 9
   Vocabulary 10
   Handwriting 11

Records of Achievement
   Comprehension and Writing 12
   Sentence and Word Skills 13

Term 1

- Key Concepts 1–7   14

Unit 1 Playing in the Park   16
   Copymaster 1 In the Park   18
   Copymaster 2 Capital Letters   19

Unit 2 On Holiday   20
   Copymaster 1 Writing Postcards   22
   Copymaster 2 *oo* words   23

Unit 3 Funnybones   24
   Copymaster 1 What Did They Say?   26
   Copymaster 2 *ar* words   27

Unit 4 I Know a Man …   28
   Copymaster 1 I Know a Man …   30
   Copymaster 2 Writing Sentences   31

Unit 5 Tank Drivers   32
   Copymaster 1 Who's Last?   34
   Copymaster 2 '*s*' words   35

Unit 6 The Stopwatch   36
   Copymaster 1 Writing a Story   38
   Copymaster 2 *i-e, ie, igh* and *y* words   39

Unit 7 The Secret of Sandy Island   40
   Copymaster 1 My Secret Island   42
   Copymaster 2 Alphabetical Ordering   43

- Assessments of Progress   44

Term 2

- Key Concepts 8–14   48

Unit 8 The Castle Rescue   50
   Copymaster 1 Story Settings   52
   Copymaster 2 My Personal Record   53

Unit 9 Sam's Dictionary   54
   Copymaster 1 Making a Dictionary   56
   Copymaster 2 *oa, o-e* and *ow* words   57

Unit 10 Three Billy Goats Gruff   58
   Copymaster 1 Winter Fun   60
   Copymaster 2 What Are They Doing?   61

Unit 11 The Little Sister's Tale   62
   Copymaster 1 People I Know   64
   Copymaster 2 What Did They Do?   65

Unit 12 In Daisy's Secret Drawer   66
   Copymaster 1 My Favourite Poem   68
   Copymaster 2 *ch, th* or *sh*?   69

Unit 13 In Hospital   70
   Copymaster 1 At the Dentist   72
   Copymaster 2 *ew, u-e, oo* words   73

Unit 14 Growing a Sunflower   74
   Copymaster 1 Flow Diagrams   76
   Copymaster 2 *al* words   77

- Assessments of Progress   78

Term 3

- Key Concepts 15–20   82

Unit 15 Goldilocks   84
   Copymaster 1 A Story Plan   86
   Copymaster 2 *a-e* words   87

Unit 16 Teeth   88
   Copymaster 1 Food I Like   90
   Copymaster 2 *a-e, ai* and *ay* words   91

Unit 17 Lofty the Giant   92
   Copymaster 1 I have read …   94
   Copymaster 2 *ir, ur* and *er* words   95

Unit 18 Who am I?   96
   Copymaster 1 Riddles   98
   Copymaster 2 *ou* and *ow* words   99

Unit 19 Moving People   100
   Copymaster 1 Sorting Information   102
   Copymaster 2 *ss, ff, ll* endings   103

Unit 20 Days of the Week   104
   Copymaster 1 My Own Poem   106
   Copymaster 2 Proper Nouns   107

- Assessments of Progress   108

Appendix 1: Spelling Specials   112
Appendix 2: Handwriting Practice Course   114
   There are 15 handwriting copymasters

Introduction

On Target English – A target-based approach to English teaching

On Target English is premised on the assumption that schools are anxious to:
- ensure the key requirements of the curricular documents have been delivered
- ensure all their children are given the opportunity to fulfil their writing potential and, in England, Wales and Northern Ireland, to ensure as many as possible achieve at least level 4 by Year 6, and in Scotland that they reach level D by P7
- ensure that teachers spend as much time teaching and as little time in preparation as possible.

At a time when ever more complex programmes are appearing for the teaching of English, On Target English (OTE) is offered as the structured and systematic, skills-based course for use by the busy teacher who quite simply wishes to maximise the overall writing performance of their children. Many teachers have been asking why many of the new literacy programmes appear so complex. OTE aims to demonstrate that effective teaching of English does not need to be complicated!

While it is becoming clear that at the national level reading skills are showing a considerable improvement, writing skills are still lagging behind. Several reasons have been offered for this, and OTE has specifically been written and produced to address these.

- **OTE is designed to boost levels of achievement.**
  Too many children are failing to achieve their full potential, often due to under-confidence and consequential lack of personal motivation. The gentle, steady progression of OTE combats this, giving even the least successful children a chance to increase their own expectations of what they are capable of achieving.

- **OTE has a systematic and structured approach.**
  It is suggested that there is currently too little direct teaching of the basic skills of writing, including grammar, spelling and punctuation. The carefully paced units provide a gradual and logical progression, whilst ensuring through essential though discrete revision, consolidation of the key writing competencies.

- **OTE challenges your pupils differentially.**
  Different levels of challenge can be offered for each pupil through the unique 'challenge flap' concept, designed to conceal or reveal the learning support boxes.

- **OTE sets clear learning targets for the pupils.**
  Each section of each unit has a specific learning target to which the child can be directed. These match, in terms addressed to the children, all the significant teaching objectives which the main curricular documents describe.

- **OTE is premised on the importance of effective classroom teaching.**
  OTE hopes to reduce the need for unreasonable amounts of pre-lesson preparation. The combination of the richly motivating Interactive Big Book, leading into accessible and uncomplicated parallel pupil texts (one for text level work and one for related sentence and word skills work) and the brief but supportive notes in the Teacher's Resource Book, ensures that a positive start to each lesson can be followed with straightforward group and/or independent work.

Main features and benefits of On Target English

Interactive Big Book

- Full colour, highly illustrated Interactive Big Book for each year group, providing a stimulating introduction for whole class and group teaching.
- Each unit has a double-page spread with all or significant extracts of the text from the pupil materials, providing opportunities for shared reading and ideal starting points for sentence and word skills activities. Most units also have extension development opportunities built in.
- The double-page spread format makes for easy management of teaching objectives, and for pupil confidence building.

Pupil books

- Closely integrated activities and organisation, with the same themes across both pupil books, and identical page numbering for ease of classroom management.
- The Challenge Flaps allow for discrete differentiation within the class, with the teacher and child agreeing to conceal or reveal the learning support boxes to any given exercise.

- Learning support boxes on every page: Helpful Words boxes and Tip boxes which make helpful suggestions, and Remember boxes, which remind children of rules already learnt. Children can refer to these before or after undertaking the exercises.
- Clear, uncluttered and child-friendly layout and 'density' of material.
- Structured and systematic sequencing of activities, giving security and enabling pupils to get on task with minimal potential for confusion and minimum teacher input.
- Learning target clearly identified for each activity, giving focus to work and encouraging child to share responsibility for own learning.

Comprehension and Writing Skills
- Full range of fiction and non-fiction text types, chosen for impact and stimulus, but also accessibility to the less fluent.
- Comprehension – giving balance of literal, inferential and evaluative exercises through the course.
- Writing composition tasks with purpose and structure, with the second activity for extension and for the quick-finishers.

Sentence and Word Skills
- All work related back to the text passage from the Interactive Big Book and the parallel unit in the Comprehension and Writing Skills book.
- Easy to follow progression through:
  grammar awareness
  punctuation/sentence construction
  Spelling
  vocabulary
  handwriting.
- Ample 'over-learning' and revision of the basic concepts to build confidence and ensure greater success.

Teacher's Resource Book
- Uncomplicated explanations of the key concepts with related teaching suggestions.
- Homework ideas for each unit.
- Spelling practice lists, graded and covering all the frequently used and important words in children's writing.
- A full range of handwriting copymasters for Years 3 and 4.
- Optional support copymasters for the child who needs a little extra help.
- Planning and classroom management support: key concept reference charts to support revision; record of achievement charts for class, groups or individual children.
- Key writing frames and copiable material from pupil texts.
- Ample tests and assessment practice.

Using the Teacher's Resource Book

Key Concept Reference Charts
Whilst the content of On Target English has been carefully arranged to meet the requirements of the main curricular documents, all teachers will, from time to time, want to refer back or forwards when teaching a particular skill.

These charts are scope and sequence charts and indicate the detail of a concept taught at the particular year, and note in which units elsewhere in the course the concepts are developed.

The skills are organised within six charts:
– Writing
– Grammar
– Sentence construction and punctuation
– Spelling
– Vocabulary
– Handwriting.

Records of Achievement
A record sheet is available for each of the two strands of the course:
– Comprehension and Writing Skills
– Sentence and Word Skills

These offer a simple and direct way to track the teaching and learning. Each component of each unit is shaded on the record sheet, indicating the basic concepts covered in the book. It is suggested that / is used to indicate a section of work completed, and **x** when it appears to have not only been completed but throughly learnt. As the course progresses, the teacher can look out for concepts not previously fully 'internalised' by particular children, and focus her or his attention and time accordingly.

These information and record sheets can be used as an on-going record and also as a transfer document to the next class.

Teaching Notes
For convenience, these are organised on a termly basis, although they need not necessarily be used in this way. The information and teaching suggestions are broken down as follows:

Termly summary of key concepts
These highlight the most important concepts to be dealt with in the term and offer some general teaching guidance for the less-experienced teacher. They are organised under:
Text level   Fiction, Poetry, Non-fiction
Sentence level Grammar, Sentence construction and punctuation

Word level   Spelling, Vocabulary extension, Handwriting.

Individual unit teaching suggestions
These are devised to be as accessible and practical as possible, and include:
- curricular references, to set the teaching context (only the relevant text is included)
- detailed teaching suggestions, which will enable the teacher to present the material without the need for extended time-consuming and detailed preparation
- suggestions for using the Interactive Big Book to introduce a session (and for subsequent group teaching where appropriate)
- ideas for introducing or extending the pupil activities in both textbooks, together with answers to all the exercises
- homework ideas.

Optional support activities and writing frame copymasters
At no point in this course are the copymasters essential to the effective use of the programme, but where the teacher needs to provide certain children with additional support, and/or where the teacher wishes to provide for pupils who might not ordinarily be able to cope with the work being undertaken by the rest of the class, then the copymasters will be helpful.

They are also a valuable resource when children need to work in a totally unsupported context, and so are used by some schools as homework assignments.

Assessments of Progress in reading comprehension, writing and spelling
At the end of each term's units of work, teachers may wish to use the photocopiable Assessments of Progress. These have been devised to give the children the opportunity to become comfortable with the testing process, and are designed to reflect the broad approach taken by the national assessment tests in English.

Weekly Spelling Specials
These photocopiable spelling lists appear in Appendix 1 and provide the opportunity to cover a range of the more important words the child should be able to spell. In many cases there is a link between the words listed in the Spelling Specials and the spellings taught in the respective unit. However, to ensure all the more important words are covered, as suggested in the appendices to the NLS or in the NLS Word Bank, sometimes the link is of necessity tenuous or non-existent.

Handwriting Practice Course/End of key stage diagnostic assessments
The final section in the Teacher's Resource Book, Appendix 2, is either additional handwriting resource material (at years 2, 3 and 4) or additional diagnostic tests (years 5 and 6) which assess all the key skills taught over the year.

On Target English Key Concept Reference Chart: Writing

Key Concepts	Unit Reference				
	OTE 2	OTE 3	OTE 4	OTE 5	OTE 6
Narrative					
chapters/episodes		15		13	9
character	11 personal information charts	2 10	5 16	1 5 18 22	1 5 12 17
description				20	
dialogue		6			12
empathy	10 empathising with a character	7	6	17 22	
figurative language			9		
first-person account	1 own experiences 6 own experiences		6	17	
openings/endings	8 completing a story	12 18	20	1 5	
own versions	10 new story, same setting 12 own lines of poetry			3 5 9 13 18 22	8 16
paragraphs		12	6	17	12
planning		12 13 18	1 6 16	9	5 12 16
plot		2 4 9	16		5 11 12
reading log				1	
sequels	10 new story, same setting	4	20		8 9 16
sequencing	3 language of time 15 sequencing a known story	9		2 9 12	
setting	8 description	1 2 9 18	8 12		5
story language			10		
Poetry					
concrete poems				7	
convey feelings/mood etc.				12	
evaluation					15
extending	4 adding new ideas 12 own lines of poetry 20 following style		18	12 19	3 21
humour	18 riddles				
pattern			14	19	21
shape poems		3			
sound to create effects		19			
Play scripts					
		7	4	6	7
Non-fiction					
alphabetically ordered texts	9 dictionary		11		
argument		16	16 17 22	15 21	10
biographical writing					2
diagrams/charts	5 labelling 7 creating a diagram/chart 14 flow charts		11	11	12
editing				14	
explanations of process				10 11	
instructions	5 ordering instructions 7 writing instructions	8 11 14	2 7 13	4	14
messages/letters	2 postcards 7 short messages		17	15 21	22
newspaper reports			3 9	16 20	6
non-chronological reports		11	9 11 13	10	12 20
note-making	11 information charts	5 17	11	8	2
organisational devices	5 labelling	8 11 14	2 7 13	4 8 11 16	2 20
persuasive			15 21	16 21	14 18 19
recounts		20	2		
reviews	17 book review				19
summary			3 19		2 4
writing information				8 11 14	

On Target English Key Concept Reference Chart: Grammar

(*cross reference to another chart)

Key Concepts	Unit Reference				
	OTE 2	OTE 3	OTE 4	OTE 5	OTE 6
adjectives		8 10 11	8 9 10 11 12 13 16 17 22	7	3 11 18 19
adverbs			3 5 16 21 22	1 14	4 11 18 19
agreement	12 is/are 13 was/were 17 have/has		15	6 14	
audience*				9 16	
changing English					
clauses					6 8
comparatives			11	16	
connectives/conjunctions	6 time words 7 time words			18	7
dialect					
direct speech*				6	
double negatives				2 19	
editing				5	14
formal English					10
gender	15 pronouns 18 nouns		18		
negatives					9
nouns	3 common 4 common 9 nouns and verbs 20 proper 20 naming word/action word	12	18 20 22	1 11 13 14 15 21 22	1 2 8 13 15
phrases			13 21		3 11
plurals		9 13	18 19	4 6 7	
prepositions				17 20 22	5 12
pronouns	4 I 15 pronouns		16 17 19 20	12 13	1
proverbs*					8 16
purpose*					
reported speech*				1 6	
sentences	1 making sense 2 jumbled 5 making sentences 11 making sentences			10 11	18 21 22
standard English					10
tenses	10 now and then 14 now and then	4 5 6		4 5 6 21	15 17 20
verbs	8 action words 9 nouns and verbs 12 is/are 13 was/were 16 verbs 19 present, past 20 naming word/action word	1 2 3 4 5 6 7 15	1 2 4 6 7 14 15 19 20 22	1 3 8 11 15 18 21 22	4 6 8 12 15 17 19 20
word classes			22	18	
word order	2 jumbled sentences			4	
word selection		14 15		8	

On Target English Key Concept Reference Chart: Sentence Construction and Punctuation

(*cross reference to another chart)

Key Concepts	Unit Reference				
	OTE 2	OTE 3	OTE 4	OTE 5	OTE 6
abbreviations					12
agreement*	12 *is/are* 13 *was/were* 17 *has/have*	10 13			
ambiguity					
apostrophe			8 9 10 11 12	2 3 15 17 19	1 3 11 14 22
capitals	1 capitals/lower case 2 starting sentences 3 starting sentences 4 I 5 proper nouns 7 titles 8 proper nouns 11 sentences 14 summary 17 titles 20 proper nouns	1 9 10 11 19	1	2 10 14 20	1 2 11 17 22
captions					
clauses*				16	6 8
commas	9 making lists 12 commas and full stops 19 commas and full stops	4 18	2 4 6	2 3 7 12 14 20 22	4 5 11 13 19 20 22
connectives/ conjunctions*	6 time words 7 time words	17 20	14		
dialogue		5 6 7 16 17	5 7 16	22	4 7 16 22
essential words		14		1 8	21
exclamation marks		8	19	2	1
full stops	1 sentences 12 commas and full stops 18 commas and full stops	1 3 8	1 19	2 10 14 20	1 2 4 11 22
headings		10			21
letter writing		15	15	21	
lists	9 making lists				
meaning					
negatives		20	2 19		
note-making					
person (1st, 2nd, 3rd)					
possessives					14
question marks	6 question sentences	2 3 8	3 19	2 14	1 2 11
questions	15 questions and answers 16 questions and answers 18 questions from statements	2	3 18		1 2 11 18
semicolon+dash				9	
speech bubbles	10 speech bubbles	5	5		
speech marks	13 speech marks	6 7 16 18	5 6 21	6 10 14 20 22	4 7 16 22
statements	18 questions from statements				1 2
time	6 time words 7 time words				
word deletion		14			10
word order	2 jumbled sentences		13		9

On Target English Key Concept Reference Chart: Spelling

(*cross reference to another chart)

Key Concepts	Unit Reference				
	OTE 2	OTE 3	OTE 4	OTE 5	OTE 6
analogy		1 4 9 20			22
apostrophes*		12	8 9 10 11 12	3	3 14
common endings		1	11 21	12 13	2 10 17 18 22
compound words	5 word sums 8 word sums		18	6	5
digraphs	2 oo 3 ar 4 sh 6 ie/y (+i-e) 7 ng 8 (+o-e) 9 oa/oe/ow 10 th 11 ee/ea 12 ch 13 ue/ew (+u-e) 17 ir/ur/er 18 ou/ow	4 5 6 7 8 10 11 12 14 16 17 20	1 4 8 9 10		
dictionaries		14 17		15 20	3 12 19
high-frequency words		App2		13	
homophones			7	11	20 various
letter strings	5 st 7 nk 14 al 19 ss/ff/ll	1 4 9 12 15 18 19 20	5 11 13 15 17	1 3 5 9 13	2 7 10 11 18 22
mnemonics					14 19
plurals	2 +s	9	18 19	4 6 7	15
prefixes	14 un 19 dis	2	12	2 15	4 6 11 14
roots	3 family words		14 19		6
rules and conventions		19		3 4 5 6 7 9 14 16 17	8 9 10 11 15 16 20
same sound/different spelling		4 7 8 12 14			20
same spelling/different sound		16	16 18	10 12	20 22
silent letters		13		19	5 21
suffixes	10 ing 15 ly 17 ed	5 7 10 11 15 19	2 3 6 12 20 22	8 14 17 18 21 22	1 6 8 9 10 13 16 18
syllables		8	5		
tenses	10 now and then 14 now and then		6		
unstressed vowels					2 17
vowel/consonant letters	1 vowel letter 6 alphabet 7 alphabet 20 vowels and consonants				
words in words		3			

On Target English Key Concept Reference Chart: Vocabulary

(*cross reference to another chart)

Key Concepts	Unit Reference				
	OTE 2	OTE 3	OTE 4	OTE 5	OTE 6
agreement				16 18 20	
alphabet	**6** alphabet sequence **7** alphabet ordering	14	1 6		12
antonyms	**11** opposites **20** opposites	2 13	7	4 9 12 14	18
apostrophes		12	17	3	
argument				10	
borrowed words			19		11
colour words	**4** colours				
compound words	**5** word sums **8** word sums		3 15 18	6	5
definitions		3	2 5 11		
dialogue		6 16		1 14	9
dictionary use		14 17	1 6 9	13 15	3 12 19
diminutives			16		
expressions		20		2 11 22	8 15 16
gender	**15** pronouns **18** nouns		14		
homonyms/homophones		18	22	19	20
new words			20		1 2 3 7 13 22
onomatopoeia				10	
prefixes	**14** un **19** dis		12	5	4 6 11 14
puzzles					16 21
rhyme	**1** rhyme words				
roots	**3** family words				
suffixes	**10** ing **15** ly **17** ed	5 7 11 15 19	4 12 13 21	5 14	1 6 8 9 10 13 16 18
synonyms	**16** synonyms	3 6 16	10	4 7	4 6 18
technical terms				8	

On Target English Key Concept Reference Chart: Handwriting

(*cross reference to another chart)

Key Concepts	Unit Reference				
	OTE 2	OTE 3	OTE 4	OTE 5	OTE 6
diagonal joins to letters without ascenders	1 an 2 en 3 ar 4 in 5 am 6 is 7 ea	8 9 10	2 5 7 8 14 18 19 20		
horizontal joins to letters without ascenders	8 on 9 oa 10 ow 11 or 12 wi 13 we 14 wa	11 12 13	1 4 11 13 15 18 20		
diagonal joins to letters with ascenders	15 at 16 et 17 it 18 al 19 cl 20 il	14 15 16	9 15 17 18 19 22		
horizontal joins to letters with ascenders		1 2 3 4 5 6 7 17 18 19 20	3 11		
size, proportion and spacing consistency		3 4 5 6 7 19	6 10 12 16 21		
speed development			4 5		
presentational skills			12 16 21		

Note: Most practice is undertaken in conjunction with spelling patterns. (See NLS Year 2 objective.)

On Target English 2 — Record of Achievement: Comprehension and Writing

Name _____

Key Concepts	UNITS																			
	1	2	3	4	5	6	7	8	9	10	11	12	13	14	15	16	17	18	19	20
comprehension																				
literal	■	■	■	■	■	■	■	■	■	■	■	■	■	■	■	■	■	■	■	■
narrative:																				
own version										■		■								
first person account	■						■													
setting								■												
character												■								
openings/endings								■												
sequencing			■												■					
sequels										■										
empathy										■										
poetry:																				
humour																		■		
extending				■								■								■
non-fiction:																				
instructions					■		■													
diagrams/charts														■						
messages/letters		■				■														
reviews																	■			
note-making											■									
organisational devices					■															■

Comments

_____

_____

_____

_____

_____

(Suggested completion: **/** = activity completed; **X** = activity fully understood.)

On Target English 2
Record of Achievement: Sentence and Word Skills

Name _____

Key Concepts	UNITS																			
	1	2	3	4	5	6	7	8	9	10	11	12	13	14	15	16	17	18	19	20
grammar:																				
agreement												▓	▓			▓				
connectives/conjunctions						▓	▓													
gender															▓		▓			
nouns			▓	▓					▓										▓	
pronouns				▓											▓					
sentences	▓	▓			▓						▓									
tenses										▓			▓							
verbs							▓	▓				▓				▓			▓	
word order		▓																		
sentence construction and punctuation:																				
agreement												▓	▓			▓				
capitals	▓	▓		▓				▓			▓			▓			▓			▓
commas								▓			▓		▓					▓		
connectives/conjunctions*						▓														
full stops		▓	▓									▓	▓							
lists										▓										
question marks						▓														
questions						▓									▓	▓				
speech bubbles										▓										
speech marks													▓							
statements																	▓			
time						▓	▓													
word order		▓																		
spelling:																				
compound words					▓		▓													
diagraphs		▓	▓	▓		▓		▓	▓	▓		▓	▓	▓		▓	▓	▓	▓	
letter strings					▓										▓				▓	
plurals		▓																		
prefixes					▓										▓				▓	
roots				▓																
suffixes										▓					▓		▓			
tenses										▓				▓						
vowel/consonant letters	▓		▓		▓		▓													▓
vocabulary:																				
alphabet						▓														
antonyms											▓									▓
colour words				▓																
compound words					▓		▓													
gender															▓		▓			
prefixes															▓				▓	
rhyme	▓																			
roots			▓																	
suffixes										▓					▓		▓			
synonyms															▓					

Comments

_____

_____

_____

(Suggested completion: / = activity completed; **X** = activity fully understood.)

On Target English © Hilary Frost 2001

Term 1 Key Concepts: Units 1–7

These notes give an overview of the key features of the term's work, and offer broad suggestions. For more detailed information on organising and delivering each unit, see the individual unit notes which follow.

Text level

Fiction – narrative

- **time and sequential relationships**
When children begin to plan simple story writing, it can help if they are able to order the events rather than introduce them haphazardly. This can be encouraged by discussion of events which have a strong time-frame element, e.g. the events in the classroom through a period of time. Help the children to think about the language they might use to indicate time is passing, e.g. when I had finished …, after a short while …, suddenly … .

- **reasons for events**
Encourage children to begin to ask questions about stories they read, or that are read to them. Why do characters do things? Why do particular events occur?

Poetry

- **word combinations and sound patterns**
Begin to make class collections or an anthology of favourite poems, focusing on poems with strong rhyme and rhythm. Make collections of rhyming words, which will also assist in spelling activities, that the children can call upon when writing their own verses.

Non-fiction

- **writing simple instructions**
Collect simple instructions for such things as making something, playing a game, recipes etc. Note their common style, which normally begins with a statement of what is to be achieved, is impersonal and is sequential – often numbered. These can then provide useful models for the children's own efforts.

- **diagrams**
Most children will find it quite difficult to draw diagrams, as opposed to pictures. However, encourage their efforts and suggest that diagrams are simplified pictures, with only the essential details, and often with labels, captions and possibly a key (or code) to help the reader understand what is intended. Their value lies in conveying information which might otherwise require extensive description to give the same amount of information.

Sentence level

Grammar

- **connectives**
Related to the text level work, introduce words and phrases that link sentences, giving writing a sense of flow and cohesion. Such words include: after, meanwhile, during, before, then, next, after a while.

Sentence construction and punctuation

- **demarcating sentences**
Constant work will be required to consolidate the concept of a sentence as a unit of language that makes sense on its own. All sentences begin with a capital letter, and it can be helpful to suggest that all sentences must end with a full stop. The fact that the question mark and exclamation mark can be used in place of a full stop can be covered by showing that each of these two punctuation marks has a full stop built into it.

- **questions**
Work on question sentences and question marks is often best delivered in the context of comparing them with statements, which end with a full stop.

- **capitalisation**
As well as at the beginning of sentences, capitals are needed as the initial letter in proper nouns and in titles, both concepts being introduced in the following units.

Word level

Phonics, graphic knowledge and spelling

- **common letter strings**
As part of the mixed diet that characterises effective teaching of phonological awareness and spelling, teaching and learning some of the common letter strings is important. It is recommended that lists displaying letter strings are collected and displayed on the wall, and whenever a new word is encountered during class or group work it is added to the chart on the wall – giving an opportunity to revisit those already in the list.

- **vowel phonemes**
Particular attention should be given to the teaching and/or consolidation of the 'long' and 'short' vowel phonemes. Some are covered in the following units,

but space does not permit a complete coverage. It is strongly recommended that where the same phoneme (sound) can be represented by different graphemes (letter groups), e.g. i-e, ie, y, igh, then each is taught and practised separately before being brought together.

- **suffixes**

The basic suffixes (word endings) should be used to help the children to understand that words are built from a combination of 'parts', e.g. the addition of 's' to signify plurals of nouns, and the addition of 'ed' and 'ing' to indicate the tenses of verbs.

Vocabulary extension

- **individual word lists**

The children should be helped to begin to keep lists of frequently used words. The words introduced in the Spelling Special (see Appendix 1) can form the backbone of such a list since they are selected from words most frequently written by children of this age.

Handwriting

- **joins**

Having been developing letter forms that lend themselves to joining, we now need to begin to encourage the children to actually join the letters in words. To this end the main joins are covered in this book, with the first seven units focusing on diagonal joins to letters without ascenders. Whenever possible, the handwriting patterns are linked to the teaching of letter strings which will be helpful with spelling.

Unit 1 — Playing in the Park

Curriculum references

England (Year 2 Term 1)
Range: Stories with familiar settings
Objectives:

> Text level work
> 4 to understand time and sequential relationships in stories
> 5 to identify and discuss reasons for events in stories
> 6 to discuss familiar story themes and link to own experiences
> 10 to use story structure to write about own experiences in same/similar form

> Sentence level work
> 4 to reread own writing for sense and punctuation

> Word level work
> 12 to begin using and practising the four basic handwriting joins:
> • diagonal joins to letters without ascenders

Wales
Range – Pupils should be given opportunities to:
2 experiment and attempt independently to communicate in writing using letters and known words
3 write in response to a variety of stimuli, including … personal experience
Skills
2 understand the difference between print and pictures, understanding the connections between speech and writing, and learn about the different purposes and functions of written language
3 to recognise the alphabetic nature of writing and discriminate between letters
4 write independently on subjects that are of interest to them
7 punctuate:
• punctuate their writing, be consistent in their use of capital letters, full stops …
8 spell:
• use their knowledge of sound–symbol relationships and phonological patterns
• recognise and use simple spelling patterns
• write common letter strings with familiar and common words
9 develop their handwriting:
• build on their knowledge of letter formation to join letters in words

Scotland (AT/PoS Level A/B)
Personal writing – Write briefly and in an appropriate sequence about a personal experience, giving an indication of feelings, using adequate vocabulary.
Punctuation and structure – Use capital letters and full stops correctly.
Handwriting – Form letters and space words legibly in linked script.
Knowledge about language – Understand and use the terms: capital, full stop, sentence.

Northern Ireland
Purpose – describe; report
Range – simple records of observations; descriptions of people or places
Expected outcomes:
• use the conventional ways of forming letter shapes in upper and lower case
• use basic punctuation conventions, including capital letters, full stops

On Target English

Interactive Big Book
• Use the picture to prompt consideration of cause and effect, there being several incidents which are likely to lead to a reaction or effect.
• Share experiences of children who have recently visited a park and compare with the incidents depicted.
• Ask volunteers to find words depicted which can be grouped as rhyming sets, e.g.
cat bat hat rat mat
band hand sand
net jet something 'wet'
leg peg
bin tin
mop 'pop' from a bottle
sock lock rock
fox box
dog log frog
'cut' on a leg hut nut

Comprehension and Writing Skills
What is happening?
The cloze passage requires literal responses to the pictures and sentence captions. Copymaster 1 from this unit provides additional support requiring children to identify what is happening in a picture.
What happens next?
This cloze passage requires literal responses to the pictures indicating the consequences of some of the incidents in the original picture/caption story.
When I go to the park
Clearly the majority of children will require some preliminary class or group work to support this writing task in which they are either reflecting on recent experiences or imagining what they might like to do during a visit to a park.

Teacher's Resource Book 2

Unit 1

ANSWERS

Comprehension
What is happening?
Ross is talking to Harry.
Beth and Ravi are feeding the ducks.
Mrs May is walking her dog.
What happens next?
The swing hits Ross and Harry.
The ducks eat the bread.
Mrs May falls over.

Sentence and Word Skills
Making sense
Revise with the class the need for a sentence to make sense in its own right. Also remind the children that sentences need to begin with a capital and end with a full stop (or question mark or exclamation mark). Offer the children some oral examples of sentences and phrases that are not sentences, and invite them to spot the 'non-sentences'.
Capital letters
Revise the differences between capital and lower case letters. Suggest that capitals are usually given the more important jobs, leading the smaller, lower case, letters in sentences, names etc. (Copymaster 2 from this unit extends this exercise.)
Vowels
There are five vowel letters (a, e, i, o, u) and one 'semi-vowel' (y), which occasionally takes the place of 'i'. Write a range of words on the board and ask volunteers to come forward and circle the vowel letters. Notice that there may sometimes be more than one vowel letter, but there are never none. If appropriate discuss the two sounds each letter can represent (the short and the long sound); note that in some regional dialects some vowel letters can represent more than two sounds (phonemes), e.g. a as in bat, bake, path.
Rhyming words
Ensure that before undertaking this task, the children have shared and discussed the Interactive Big Book picture.

ANSWERS

Sentence work
Making sense
1 Mrs May has a dog.
   He is called Scruff.
   He is little and scruffy.
2 individual answers

Capital letters
1 A G Q B P L
2 D E K B M W R
3 individual answers

Word work
Vowels
sun van net pin
cut mop bag hut
Rhyming words
individual answers

Homework suggestions
- Ask the children to write two sentences about their home, each beginning with a capital letter and ending with a full stop.
- Copy five words from a cereal packet (or similar) and circle the vowel letters.

17

In the Park

What are they doing?

> sliding   swinging   eating a picnic
> playing football   paddling

Objective: To identify what is happening

Capital Letters

Copy the letters and match the frogs to their lily pads.

Objective: To write capital letters

Unit 2 On Holiday

Curriculum references

England (Year 2 Term 1)
Range: Stories with familiar settings
Objectives:

Text level work
6 to discuss familiar themes and link to own experiences
10 to write about own experiences in same/similar form

Sentence level work
4 to reread own writing for sense and punctuation
5 to revise knowledge about other uses of capitalisation, e.g. for names, and begin to use in own writing

Word level work
2 to revise and extend the reading and spelling of words containing the long vowel phonemes
7 to use word endings, e.g. 's' (plural)
12 to begin using and practising the four basic handwriting joins:
• diagonal joins to letters without ascenders

Wales
Range – Pupils should be given opportunities to:
3 write in response to a variety of stimuli, including personal experience
4 write in a range of forms, incorporating some of the characteristics of those forms
Skills
1 write with confidence, fluency and accuracy
2 understand the difference between print and pictures ... and learn about the different purposes and functions of written language
4 write independently on subjects that are of interest to them
5 identify the purpose for which they write
7 punctuate:
• punctuate their writing, be consistent in their use of capital letters, full stops
8 spell:
• use their knowledge of sound–symbol relationships and phonological patterns
• recognise and use simple spelling patterns
• spell words with common suffixes
9 develop their handwriting:
• build on their knowledge of letter formation to join letters in words

Scotland (AT/PoS Level A/B)
Personal writing – Write briefly and in an appropriate sequence about a personal experience, giving an indication of feelings, using adequate vocabulary.
Punctuation and structure – Use capital letters and full stops correctly ... and use common linking words: and, but, then, so, that.

Spelling – Spell frequently used words accurately through using a simple wordbank or dictionary. The learning of spelling rules should support this.
Handwriting – Form letters and space words legibly in linked script.
Knowledge about language – Understand and use the terms: capital, full stop, sentence.

Northern Ireland
Purpose – express thoughts and feelings; describe
Range – letters
Expected outcomes:
- use conventional ways of forming letter shapes in upper and lower case
- use basic punctuation conventions, including capital letters, full stops

On Target English

Interactive Big Book
- Discuss how postcards give the opportunity for short, friendly messages without the need for a long letter, and also have the advantage of the pictorial component. Use this to discuss how pictures and words can often complement each other.
- Use the picture sequence of the postcard being sent, delivered and read to extend the notion of cause and effect from the previous unit.

Comprehension and Writing Skills
It is true?
The cloze passage requires literal responses to the postcard, with the child copying only the 'true' sentences.
Picture clues
This cloze passage requires literal responses to the picture.
A card for Granny
Discuss what the children might wish to put into a message on a postcard to Granny. Then, on a separate sheet or using the frame on copymaster 1 from this unit, encourage them to write two or three sentences about the holiday. This can either be the children recalling their own experiences of a holiday or writing as if they are one of the children in the illustrations.

ANSWERS

Comprehension
Is it true?
The sea is cold.
Jack will see Misha soon.
Picture clues
Misha stuck a stamp on the card.
She put the postcard in a postbox.
A postman took it to Jack's house.

Unit 2

Sentence and Word Skills

Jumbled sentences
Revise with the class the need for a sentence to make sense in its own right. Also remind the children that sentences need to begin with a capital and end with a full stop (or question mark or exclamation mark). Then talk about the importance of words being written in the correct order. Write a simple jumbled sentence on the board and invite a volunteer to read the words and suggest the correct order for the words.

Using capital letters
Revise the differences between capital and lower case letters. Remind the children that capitals are usually given the more important jobs, leading the smaller, lower case, letters in sentences, names etc.

oo words
This work on the long 'oo' sound gives the opportunity to talk about how different letter combinations can often make the same sound, e.g. oo in boot and ue in blue. Also, if the children are ready, introduce the idea that a letter or combination of letters can make different sounds, e.g. oo in boot (long) and in good (short). Copymaster 2 from this unit gives an opportunity to practise these alongside each other.

Adding s
Discuss that if we want to write about more than one thing we normally add an 's' to the word. Draw a picture on the board (e.g. a bird) and label it. Now draw two birds and invite a volunteer to label it, drawing to the children's attention the differences between the two words, i.e. the addition of a suffix. Use your discretion as to whether it is appropriate yet to begin to use the terms 'plural' and 'suffix' with this group/class.

Adding s
5 hens 3 balls 1 hoop 2 hats
7 mops 3 caps 5 spoons 1 dog

Homework suggestions
- Collect words with the oo letter pattern, and (if appropriate) list them in two groups according to the sound of the oo.
- Write a sentence (or more) about something which was most enjoyable about the last school holiday.

ANSWERS

Sentence work

Jumbled sentences
1. The sun is hot.
   It is fun on the beach.
   Misha plays on the sand.
   Then she goes into the sea.
   The sea is cold.
2. individual answers

Using capital letters
1. We like ice lollies.
   It is hot today.
   My mum is asleep.
   Gran is flying my kite.
2. individual answers

Word work

oo words
Answers might include:
stool: tool pool fool cool spool
boot: hoot root shoot scoot
spoon: moon soon noon

Year 2 Unit 2 Copymaster 1

Name _____ **Date** _____

Writing Postcards

Draw a picture for your card.

Objective: To write a postcard

On Target English © Hilary Frost 2001

oo words

Finish these word sums:

h + oot = __hoot__   l + ook = __look__

f + ood = _____   c + ook = _____

sc + oot = _____   h + ook = _____

sh + oot = _____   b + ook = _____

m + oon = _____   t + ook = _____

n + oon = _____   br + ook = _____

s + oon = _____   cr + ook = _____

sp + oon = _____   sh + ook = _____

r + oom = _____   s + oot = _____

br + oom = _____   f + oot = _____

Choose a word you have made to rhyme with each of these words:

shoot _____   soon _____   room _____

book _____   foot _____   shook _____

      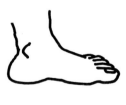

Objective: To learn to spell words with *oo*

Unit 3 Funnybones

Curriculum references

England (Year 2 Term 1)
Range: Stories with familiar settings
Objectives:

Text level work
4 to understand time and sequential relationships in stories, i.e. what happened when
11 to use the language of time to structure a sequence of events

Sentence level work
2 to find examples … of words and phrases that link sentences
4 to reread own writing for sense and punctuation
5 to revise knowledge about other uses of capitalisation, e.g. for names, and begin to use in own writing

Word level work
3 the common spelling patterns for the vowel phoneme: ar
10 new words from reading linked to particular topics, to build individual collections of personal interest or significant words
12 to begin using and practising the four basic handwriting joins:
• diagonal joins to letters without ascenders

Wales
Range – Pupils should be given opportunities to:
2 experiment and attempt independently to communicate in writing using letters and known words
3 write in response to a variety of stimuli, including stories
4 write in a range of forms, incorporating some of the characteristics of those forms; the range should include a variety of narratives, e.g. stories
Skills
2 understand the difference between print and pictures, understanding the connections between speech and writing
7 punctuate:
• punctuate their writing, be consistent in their use of capital letters, full stops
8 spell:
• use their knowledge of sound–symbol relationships and phonological patterns
• recognise and use simple spelling patterns
• write common letter strings with familiar and common words
• spell commonly occurring simple words
9 develop their handwriting:
• build on their knowledge of letter formation to join letters in words

Scotland (AT/PoS Level A/B)
Imaginative writing – Write a brief imaginative story, with discernible organisation and using adequate vocabulary.
Punctuation and structure – Use capital letters and full stops correctly … and use common linking words.
Spelling – Spell frequently used words accurately through using a simple wordbank or dictionary.
Handwriting – Form letters and space words legibly in linked script.
Knowledge about language – Understand and use the terms: letter, word, capital, full stop, sentence.

Northern Ireland
Purpose – develop imagination; narrate
Range – stories
Expected outcomes:
• use conventional ways of forming letter shapes in upper and lower case
• spell recognisably a range of familiar and important words
• use basic punctuation conventions, including capital letters, full stops
• write correctly structured sentences

On Target English

Interactive Big Book
• Focus on the words that are actually spoken. Draw attention to the implications of sequencing of events that is implied, and draw on the board a simple diagram with arrows, i.e. 1 skeletons talking 2 putting on dog's lead 3 someone being scared.
• Revise the term 'noun' for naming words. Ask the children to suggest the nouns they can identify in the picture.
• Discuss the speech bubbles containing the words that were actually spoken. Then relate this to the text in the Comprehension and Writing Skills book (page 10), in which the words are shown in a different way from on a picture, i.e. between speech marks, because speech bubbles in text passages wouldn't be practical.
• Ask the children to suggest the 'ar words' they can identify in the picture, i.e. car, park, star, scarf.

Comprehension and Writing Skills
What's missing?
The cloze exercise requires literal responses to the passage.
Picture clues
This cloze passage requires rather more extensive literal responses to the passage, drawing out the sequencing implied by the text.

Unit 3

What did the skeletons do next?
Talk through the picture story and sequence of events. Brainstorm what might have happened next – possibly arriving at several options from which the children can select when undertaking the activity either as a group or independently. Copymaster 1 from this unit is an extra activity.

ANSWERS

Comprehension
What's missing?
In the dark dark town there was a dark dark street. Down the dark dark staircase there was a dark dark cellar.
And in the dark dark cellar … some skeletons lived. There was a big skeleton, a little skeleton and a dog skeleton.
Talking skeletons!
(The use of correct speech punctuation should not be an issue at this stage.)
First the big skeleton asked, "What shall we do tonight?"
The little skeleton answered, "Let's take the dog for a walk and frighten somebody!"
Then the big skeleton said, "Good idea!"

Sentence and Word Skills
Naming words
Revise the term 'noun', i.e. naming word. Place several objects in front of the group and ask the children to give you a noun for each. Then ask the children to look around the classroom and identify other 'naming words', or nouns.
Capital letters and full stops
The ever important task of teaching sentence punctuation and structure continues here. Ask the children to remind you of the three golden rules of writing a sentence, i.e. 1 It must make sense. 2 It must begin with a capital. 3 It must end with a full stop (or question mark or exclamation mark).
ar words
'ar' is a common digraph and one of those worth focusing on in the early stages of a structured spelling programme. The following list can be used for structuring related spelling activities, especially work based on onset and rime:
bar car far jar tar star scar
ark bark dark lark mark park shark spark
arm farm harm
art cart dart part tart start smart
barn darn yarn
card hard lard yard
harp scarp sharp
scarf
harsh marsh
The are sound (as in care) is an important 'exception' to begin to be aware of, but most children will be more ready to deal with it a little later.

The related task on copymaster 2 from this unit, leads to looking for words inside words (e.g. <u>bar</u>k). Also, some children will enjoy making rhyming couplets (e.g. Twinkle, twinkle little star …).
Family words
If they aren't already being used, now might be an opportune time to begin making word lists and/or individual spelling logs in which significant and frequently used words can be written. Organise these alphabetically, thus extending and reinforcing the activities on the alphabet from earlier units.

ANSWERS

Sentence work
Naming words
1 skeleton cat bike
   house bin rat
2 The skeleton rode a bike.
   A dog chased the skeleton.
Capital letters and full stops
The big skeleton lived in a cellar.
It was a very dark cellar.
He lived with a small skeleton.
The two skeletons had a dog.

Word work
ar words
Answers might include:
car arm star jar card scarf park
Family words
1 brother   2 father   3 mother   4 sister

Homework suggestions
- Write five nouns found in the bedroom.
- Collect words with the ar letter pattern.

What Did They Say?

Objective: To write dialogue

ar words

Write the words that rhyme. Colour the pictures.

| car | dark | jar | bar | park |
| far | bark | tar | lark | star |

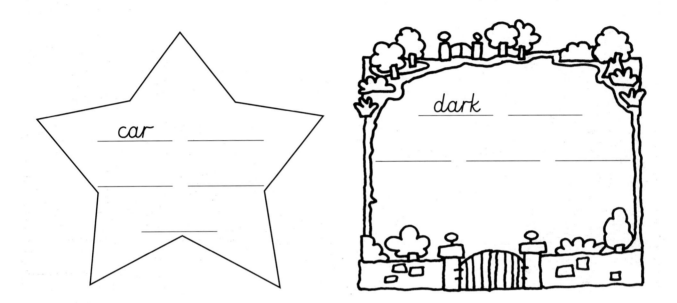

Sort these words into rhyming families.

| bar | card | cart | car | hard | dart |
| lard | tart | star | jar | yard | start |

ar words   *ard* words   *art* words

Objective: To learn to spell words with *ar*

Unit 4 I Know a Man ...

Curriculum references

England (Year 2 Term 1)
Range: Stories with familiar settings
Objectives:

Text level work
7 to learn, reread and recite favourite poems, taking account of punctuation; to comment on aspects such as word combinations, sound patterns and forms of presentation
12 to use simple poetry structures and to substitute own ideas, write new lines

Sentence level work
5 to revise knowledge about other uses of capitalisation, e.g. for names, and begin to use in own writing

Word level work
10 new words from reading linked to particular topics, to build individual collections of personal interest or significant words
12 to begin using and practising the four basic handwriting joins:
- diagonal joins to letters without ascenders

Wales
Range – Pupils should be given opportunities to:
3 write in response to a variety of stimuli, including poems
4 write in a range of forms, incorporating some of the characteristics of those forms; the range should include a variety of poems
7 make choices about vocabulary and organise imaginative and factual writing in different ways, e.g. a cumulative pattern in a poem
Skills
7 punctuate:
- punctuate their writing, be consistent in their use of capital letters
8 spell:
- use their knowledge of sound–symbol relationships and phonological patterns
- recognise and use simple spelling patterns
9 develop their handwriting:
- build on their knowledge of letter formation to join letters in words

Scotland (AT/PoS Level A/B)
Imaginative writing – Write a brief imaginative story or poem or dialogue, with discernible organisation and using adequate vocabulary.
Punctuation and structure – Use capital letters correctly.
Spelling – Spell frequently used words accurately through using a simple wordbank or dictionary.
Handwriting – Form letters and space words legibly in linked script.
Knowledge about language – Understand and use the terms: capital, drafting, redrafting.

Northern Ireland
Purpose – develop imagination
Range – poems
Expected outcomes:
- use the conventional ways of forming letter shapes in upper and lower case
- spell recognisably a range of familiar and important words
- use basic punctuation conventions, including capital letters
- write correctly structured sentences

On Target English

Interactive Big Book
- Discuss the rhyme structure of the poem. Write on the board the rhyming words from each couplet and then, with the children's help, list other rhyming words. Once this is done together try making up alternative (silly) lines for the poem.
- Collect and list, with the help of volunteers, as many 'sh' words as can be found in the picture.
- Identify in the colourful pictures as many colour words as possible, listing them on the board and encouraging the children to add them into their spelling logs, if they are now using these.

Comprehension and Writing Skills
Endings
The children should select the most appropriate ending for each sentence.
Funny men!
This task requires the children to copy and complete the sentences, but be sure to check that earlier lessons on the use of capitals and full stops are being remembered, as is the need for each sentence to make sense in its own right. Copymaster 2 from this unit is an additional activity.
Make your own poem
For those children for whom it is not practical for the whole poem to be copied, a version with appropriate words omitted is available as copymaster 1 from this unit.
Some children might be able to take this work further and, based on the class/group work with the Interactive Big Book (see above), write completely new lines for the poem.

Unit 4

ANSWERS

Comprehension
Endings
Mr Red wears a saucepan on his head.
Mr Black keeps peanuts in a sack.
Mr Pink fell head first in the sink.
Mr Brown rides tigers into town.
Funny men!
Mr Red wore a saucepan on his head.
Mr Blue keeps white mice in his shoe.
The nicest man was Mr Green.

Sentence and Word Skills
Nouns and silly sentences
Revise the term 'noun', i.e. naming word. Use this section of the unit to revise nouns and basic sentence structure, as well as the ee and ar vowel digraphs.
Capital I
It is not unusual to find older children who still write the personal pronoun I in lower case, so the sooner and more firmly embedded that I always needs a capital letter, the better.
sh words
'sh' is perhaps the most common consonant digraph and another of those worth focusing on in the early stages of a structured spelling programme. The following list can be used for structuring related spelling activities, especially work based on onset and rime:
sh-
sham shall shack
shed shelf shell
shin ship shift
shop shot shock
shut
-sh
ash bash cash dash gash lash mash rash sash wash
mesh
dish fish wish
cosh posh
hush rush
two-letter blend+sh
clash flash slash crash smash splash
flesh fresh
swish
blush flush plush slush brush crush
Colour words
Colour words are frequently used by children in their writing and so, if they have them, should be added to the children's word lists and/or individual spelling logs.

ANSWERS

Sentence work
Nouns and silly sentences
1 Mr Yellow keeps his car in the garage.
   He likes to eat sweets.
   He went out to pick apples off the tree.
   Mr Yellow said he saw a bright star in the sky.
2 jar cart arm
   bee weed eel
Capital I
I like funny poems.
Gran thinks I tell funny jokes.
I have a book of jokes I like.
At school I make my friends laugh.

Word work
sh words
1 shoe 2 shelf 3 shell 4 ship 5 cash 6 fish
7 crash 8 splash 9 shop
Colour words
1 blue pink yellow green
   orange black red brown
2 individual answers

Homework suggestions
- Write some rhyming couplets about animals, e.g.
  Our big fat cat
  Sleeps on the mat.
- Write two sentences about what you did yesterday, each sentence having the word I in it.

Year 2 Unit 4 Copymaster 1

Name _____ **Date** _____

I Know a Man ...

I know a man called Mr Red –

He wears a _____ on his head.

I know a man called Mr Black –

He keeps _____ in a sack.

I know a man called Mr Blue –

He keeps _____ in his shoe.

I know a man called Mr Brown –

He rides _____ into town.

I know a man called Mr Grey –

_____

Objective: To write a poem

On Target English © Hilary Frost 2001

Year 2 Unit 4 Copymaster 2

Name _____ Date _____

Writing Sentences

Write three sentences about the picture.
Remember the capitals and full stops.

1 _____
_____
2 _____
_____
3 _____
_____

Objective: To write simple sentences correctly

On Target English © Hilary Frost 2001

Unit 5 Tank Drivers

Curriculum references

England (Year 2 Term 1)
Range: Instructions
Objectives:

> **Text level work**
> 13 to read simple instructions in the classroom
> 14 to note key instructional features
> 15 to write simple instructions
> 16 to use models from reading to organise instructions sequentially
> 18 to use appropriate register in writing instructions, i.e. direct, impersonal

> **Sentence level work**
> 5 to revise knowledge about other uses of capitalisation, e.g. for names, and begin to use in own writing

> **Word level work**
> 12 to begin using and practising the four basic handwriting joins:
> • diagonal joins to letters without ascenders

Wales
Range – Pupils should be given opportunities to:
4 write in a range of forms, incorporating some of the characteristics of those forms; the range should include ... messages, e.g. instructions
7 make choices about vocabulary and organise ... factual writing in different ways
Skills
1 write with confidence, fluency and accuracy
2 ... learn about the different purposes and functions of written language
5 identify the purpose for which they write
7 punctuate:
• recognise that punctuation is essential to help a reader understand what is written
• punctuate their writing, be consistent in their use of capital letters, full stops
8 spell:
• use their knowledge of sound–symbol relationships and phonological patterns
• recognise and use simple spelling patterns
• write common letter strings with familiar and common words
• spell commonly occurring simple words
9 develop their handwriting:
• build on their knowledge of letter formation to join letters in words

Scotland (AT/PoS Level A/B)
Functional writing – Write briefly in an appropriate form for a variety of practical purposes.
Punctuation and structure – Use capital letters and full stops correctly.
Spelling – Spell frequently used words accurately through using a simple wordbank or dictionary. The learning of spelling rules should support this.
Handwriting – Form letters and space words legibly in linked script.
Knowledge about language – Understand and use the terms: capital, full stop, sentence.

Northern Ireland
Purpose – inform and explain; report
Range – to write for a variety of forms
Expected outcomes:
• use the conventional ways of forming letter shapes in upper and lower case
• spell recognisably a range of familiar and important words
• use basic punctuation conventions, including capital letters, full stops
• write correctly structured sentences

On Target English

Interactive Big Book
🍎 Draw attention to the instructions, in particular noting:
the clear statement of purpose at the beginning
sequential steps set out in a list
the use of direct language
🍎 The picture and words on the right-hand page give the opportunity to revise and practise the st letter pattern.

Comprehension and Writing Skills
Playing Tank Drivers
Here the children are given the opportunity to answer straightforward, literal-response questions using sentence answers. Use the opportunity to discuss how this should be done, and undertake the activity orally before expecting the children to work in groups or independently.
Who's last?
The cloze passage requires literal responses to the picture, and in particular to the speech bubble in the picture. Copymaster 1 from this unit is provided to give support to children for whom this task would require too much writing.
A new child
The children need to complete the sentences with reference to information gleaned from the pictures, and then to sequence the instructions correctly.
Clearing away
Diagrams often support instructions. This gives a simple introduction to how diagrams can convey information effectively.

Teacher's Resource Book 2

Unit 5

ANSWERS

Comprehension
Playing Tank Drivers
The game is called Tank Drivers.
Three or more children are needed to play.
When you hear "thick mud" you fall down.
If you do the wrong thing you are out.
Who's last?
Imran is calling the instructions.
He is saying, "Thick mud!" (Punctuation optional!)
All the children must fall down.
They are all very good but Ross is the last to fall down, so he is out.

Sentence and Word Skills
Making sentences
Another opportunity to practise essentials of sentence writing – the need for it to make sense, and the requirement for an initial capital and a final full stop.
Special naming words
The focus here is on capitals being used for proper nouns, in particular people's names and place names.
st words
Perhaps the most frequent consonant blend, and certainly one worth revisiting. Copymaster 2 from this unit broadens the practice to include other 's' blends.
Word sums
This early introduction to compound words helps the children to discover that words often have component parts, even though not usually as immediately apparent as is the case with compound words.

ANSWERS

Sentence work
Making sentences
1. It is Imran's birthday.
   Imran is having a party.
   Lots of children have come to Imran's house.
   They are playing games.
2. individual answers

Special naming words
1. individual answers
2. Salima Winston Ross Jack Manjit Leena
3. Imran Desai London Tara Suman Bombay

Word work
st words
stick star stamp
stew step stem
stream street steam
Word sums
policewoman classroom outside playground football cloakroom

Homework suggestions
- Make a list, using initial capitals, of names of family members.
- Draw a labelled diagram of your bedroom, to show where the door, window and the main items of furniture are located.

Year 2 Unit 5 Copymaster 1

Name _____ Date _____

Who's Last?

Look at the picture.

Finish these sentences. Fill in the gaps.

_____ is calling the instructions.

He is saying _____ .

All the children must _____ _____ .

They are all very good but _____ is the last to fall down, so he is _____ .

Write your own sentence about the picture.

_____

Objective: To write sentences that make sense

On Target English © Hilary Frost 2001

Year 2 Unit 5 Copymaster 2

Name _____ Date _____

's' words

The words in the box are jumbled. Sort them into their correct lists.

| spill snap stuck spend stun |
| speck stand snuggle stack swill |
| snail spell swim swish swig snob |

sp words   sw words   sn words   st words

_____   _____   _____   _____
_____   _____   _____   _____
_____   _____   _____   _____
_____   _____   _____   _____

Add two more of your own to each list:

_____   _____   _____   _____
_____   _____   _____   _____

Write the missing words:

_____   _____   _____   _____

Objective: To practise 's' blends

On Target English © Hilary Frost 2001

Unit 6 The Stopwatch

Curriculum references

England (Year 2 Term 1)
Range: Stories with familiar settings
Objectives:

Text level work
5 to identify and discuss reasons for events in stories, linked to plot
10 to use story structure to write about own experiences in same/similar form

Sentence level work
2 to find examples, in fiction and non-fiction, of words and phrases that link sentences

Word level work
2 to revise and extend the reading and spelling of words containing different spellings of the long vowel phonemes
12 to begin using and practising the four basic handwriting joins:
• diagonal joins to letters without ascenders

Wales
Range – Pupils should be given opportunities to:
3 write in response to a variety of stimuli, including stories
4 write in a range of forms, incorporating some of the characteristics of those forms; the range should include a variety of narratives, e.g. stories
Skills
1 write with confidence, fluency and accuracy
3 to recognise the alphabetic nature of writing and discriminate between letters
4 write independently on subjects that are of interest to them
7 punctuate:
• recognise that punctuation is essential to help a reader understand what is written
• punctuate their writing, be consistent in their use of capital letters, full stops and question marks
8 spell:
• write each letter of the alphabet
• use their knowledge of sound–symbol relationships and phonological patterns
• write common letter strings with familiar and common words
• spell commonly occurring simple words
9 develop their handwriting:
• build on their knowledge of letter formation to join letters in words

Scotland (AT/PoS Level A/B)
Personal writing – Write briefly and in an appropriate sequence about a personal experience, giving an indication of feelings, using adequate vocabulary.

Punctuation and structure – Use capital letters and full stops correctly ... and use common linking words.
Spelling – Spell frequently used words accurately ... The learning of spelling rules should support this.
Handwriting – Form letters and space words legibly in linked script.
Knowledge about language – Understand and use the terms: letter, word, capital, full stop, sentence.

Northern Ireland
Purpose – describe; inform and explain
Range – stories; simple records of observations
Expected outcomes:
- use the conventional ways of forming letter shapes in upper and lower case
- make use of names and order of the letters of the alphabet
- spell recognisably a range of familiar and important words
- use basic punctuation conventions, including capital letters, full stops and question marks
- write correctly structured sentences

On Target English

Interactive Big Book
- Having shared the text, draw attention to the punctuation, and in particular the end-sentence punctuation. Notice that question marks and exclamation marks have built-in full stops. If appropriate, begin to consider the relationship between the words in speech bubbles and the words inside speech marks (i.e. both being words actually spoken).

Comprehension and Writing Skills
Right order
The children need to correctly order the sentences. Be sure to check that when copied, the sentences have initial capital letters and full stops.
Endings
A literal understanding of the text is required for the children to match the correct beginnings and endings of the sentences.
Gran's lost dog
The activity is designed to help the children give sequential structure to their story writing.
Lost and found
At this point the children should be ready to use the same or a similar writing model to describe their own experience. Importantly, they are also encouraged to inform the reader of their feelings, as well as describing the events. Copymaster 1 from this unit provides support.

Teacher's Resource Book 2

Unit 6

ANSWERS

Comprehension
Right order
1 Gran gave Tom a stopwatch.
2 Jan and Tom had a staring match.
3 Tom lost his stopwatch.
4 Jan and Tom had a fight for 7 minutes.

Endings
Tom liked his stopwatch because he liked to time how long things took.
When Tom lost his stopwatch he was very upset.
Tom and Jan fought because she had taken his stopwatch.

Sentence and Word Skills
Time words
Time words are one category of connectives, linking and giving cohesion to a piece of writing. Such words are particularly important in signalling sequences.

Questions
Here the children are first introduced in this course to the nature and punctuation of question sentences. In class and group sessions, invite volunteers to make up questions on a particular subject, and to differentiate questions and statements when they are speaking about a given topic.

i-e, ie and y words
One of the important sets of long vowel phonemes. Copymaster 2 from this unit broadens the material to include the igh digraph.

The alphabet
It is important that the children become familiar with the letters of the alphabet, and begin to have an awareness of alphabetical ordering. Clearly the activities in this unit can be extended quite readily, with the children making similar tasks to those shown for each other to complete.

ANSWERS

Sentence work
Time words
When he got home Tom had tea.
After tea he had a bath.
Then he found he had lost his watch!
In the end he found his sister had it!

Questions
2 Have you seen my watch?
   Where did you put it?
   When did you have it last?

Word work
i-e, ie and y words
1 ki<u>te</u> pi<u>pe</u> pi<u>e</u> ti<u>e</u> fl<u>y</u> sk<u>y</u>

The alphabet
1 a b <u>c</u> d e <u>f</u> g h i j k <u>l</u> m n o p q r <u>s</u> t u v <u>w</u> x y z
2 A B <u>C</u> D
   G <u>H</u> I J K
   Q R S <u>T</u>
   L M <u>N</u> O
   V W X Y
   T <u>U</u> V <u>W</u>

Homework suggestions
• Write three sentences about what happened when they got home, each to include a 'time' word, showing the sequence of the events.
• Write and decorate a version of the alphabet.

Writing a Story

Story title _____

Helpful words
cat   dog   road   field   farmer   cross   pleased

Finish this story. Fill in the gaps.
Select four words from the box.

Gran lost her _____. He ran into a _____.

A _____ found him. She was very _____ to have him back.

Add one more sentence of your own.

_____

Give your story a title.

Objective: To write a story

Name _____   Date _____

i-e, *ie*, *igh* and *y* words

Underline and then copy the missing words.

| my   bike   lights   bright   night   wipe   dry   like |

It was _____ birthday.

Uncle Mike bought me a new _____.

Gran bought me some _____.

They were very _____ lights.

Now I can ride my bike at _____.

When it rains I _____ my bike.

I keep it _____ so it won't go rusty.

I _____ my bike.

Colour and number the pictures in the right order.

☐   ☐   ☐   ☐

Objective: To spell words with *i-e*, *ie*, *igh* and *y*

Unit 7 The Secret of Sandy Island

Curriculum references

England (Year 2 Term 1)
Range: Instructions
Objectives:

> **Text level work**
> 13 to read simple instructions in the classroom
> 14 to note key instructional features
> 15 to write simple instructions
> 16 to use models from reading to organise instructions sequentially
> 17 to use diagrams in instructions
> 18 to use appropriate register in writing instructions, i.e. direct, impersonal

> **Sentence level work**
> 2 to find examples, in fiction and non-fiction, of words and phrases that link sentences
> 5 to revise knowledge about other uses of capitalisation, e.g. for names, and begin to use in own writing

> **Word level work**
> 12 to begin using and practising the four basic handwriting joins:
> • diagonal joins to letters without ascenders

Wales
Range – Pupils should be given opportunities to:
3 write in response to a variety of stimuli
4 write in a range of forms, incorporating some of the characteristics of those forms; the range should include messages, e.g. instructions
Skills
2 learn about the different purposes and functions of written language
3 recognise the alphabetic nature of writing and discriminate between letters
4 write independently on subjects that are of interest to them
5 identify the purpose for which they write
7 punctuate:
• recognise that punctuation is essential to help a reader understand what is written
• punctuate their writing, be consistent in their use of capital letters, full stops and question marks, and begin to use commas
8 spell:
• write each letter of the alphabet
• use their knowledge of sound–symbol relationships and phonological patterns
• recognise and use simple spelling patterns
• write common letter strings with familiar and common words
9 develop their handwriting:
• build on their knowledge of letter formation to join letters in words

Scotland (AT/PoS Level A/B)
Functional writing – Write briefly in an appropriate form for a variety of practical purposes.
Punctuation and structure – Use capital letters and full stops correctly ... and use common linking words.
Spelling – Spell frequently used words accurately ... The learning of spelling rules should support this.
Handwriting – Form letters and space words legibly in linked script.
Knowledge about language – Understand and use the terms: letter, word, capital, full stop, sentence.

Northern Ireland
Purpose – inform and explain; report
Range – labels; captions; descriptions of people or places; diagrams
Expected outcomes:
• use the conventional ways of forming letter shapes in upper and lower case
• make use of names and order of the letters of the alphabet
• spell recognisably a range of familiar and important words
• use basic punctuation conventions, including capital letters, full stops and question marks
• write correctly structured sentences

On Target English

Interactive Big Book
• Use the picture and the diagram to help the children to recognise the relationship between map/plan and the real land form of an island.
• With reference to the picture sequence, discuss how we can use words and phrases to indicate the passing of time.

Comprehension and Writing Skills
What is the secret?
The cloze passage requires literal responses to the map and instructions.
Clues
Encourage a deductive enquiry to enable the children to respond. They should now be writing their answers in sentences.
Your own secret island
Most children will initially need considerable support for this task, both for drawing a map and for writing the instructions. Copymaster 1 from this unit will be helpful to some to structure their work. Help the children to begin to appreciate the need for the instructions to be direct, sequential and impersonal.
Treasure!
The message is another form of instruction, so the style and tone should be as detailed above.

Teacher's Resource Book 2

Unit 7

ANSWERS

Comprehension
What is the secret?
The island is called Sandy Island.
A tree is growing on the island.
The walk starts on the beach.
You find a chart in the cave.
Clues
Individual answers, based on the illustration.

Sentence and Word Skills
Time words
Time words are one category of connectives, linking and giving cohesion to a piece of writing. Such words are particularly important in signalling sequences.
Titles
The use of capitals in titles can be tricky to master, but if they learn the basic notion of using capitals for the first letter of a title and for the initial letter of each of the important words, the children will have an essential mastery of what is normally required.
ng and nk words
These two letter strings are quite frequent in short words, following a short vowel. In preparation for this activity write on the board both letter strings and in turn write each of the short vowels before each, thus creating the possible rime part of words. Then ask the children to suggest words of which the letters on the board form the 'rime', e.g. ang bang sang etc; ing sing bring etc.
The alphabet
This task provides an early introduction to alphabetical ordering. Follow it up with other sets of words that can be ordered by their first letter. The activities on copymaster 2 from this unit should also be appropriate for some children.

Homework suggestions
- Draw a map of their own imaginary island in preparation for the writing task.
- Give a group or groups of words for the children to arrange in alphabetical order by their first letters.

ANSWERS

Sentence work
Time words
individual answers
Titles
1. Alice in Wonderland
   A Big Book of Birds
   The Great Space Adventure
   Thomas Hits the Buffers
2. individual task

Word work
ng and nk words
1. wing bang rang king
   sink pink wink tank
2. individual answers
3. individual answers

The alphabet
2. beach path lake hill cave
3. beach cave hill lake path

41

Year 2 Unit 7 Copymaster 1

Name _____   **Date** _____

My Secret Island

Draw a map of your island.

Mark on your island:

a wood   a hut   hills

and a path

Write your secret message:

Objective: To draw a map and write instructions

On Target English © Hilary Frost 2001

Year 2 Unit 7 Copymaster 2

Name _____ Date _____

Alphabetical Ordering

a b c d e f g h i j k l m n o p q r s t u v w x y z

Write the alphabet in capital letters:
_____

Write these sets of letters in alphabetical order:

d a c b _____   g f i h _____
j g d b _____   t p w k _____
z a h f y _____   j t q p l _____
H L P W B _____   M Y F A K _____

Write these words in alphabetical order:

bee caterpillar ant
_____

goat horse ferret
_____

house tent flat bungalow
_____

rose buttercup daffodil tulip
_____

car lorry bus van
_____

Objective: To practise capital letters and putting words in alphabetical order

On Target English © Hilary Frost 2001

Term 1 Assessment of Progress: Comprehension

Pete and the Stick

One day, Pete was walking down the road with no one but his shadow, when he found a stick. It wasn't an ordinary kind of stick that anyone might find. It was almost a tree. It had branches growing from it, with green leaves on them, and it was very, very big.

Pete bent down to pick it up. His shadow bent down too.

Pete's stick stretched right across the pavement from one side to the other. And when Pete marched along, holding it up in the air, no one could get by. Even his shadow had to walk behind.

Everyone else had to walk on the road, which made them rather cross. But Pete didn't notice. He was an aeroplane. Weeeeee! Everyone got very quickly out of the way.

Leila Berg

Teacher's Note for spelling assessment on page 4

First, discuss the large picture and the pictures around it, ensuring the children know what each picture represents. Ask the children to write the name of each small picture in the box underneath it.
Read through the passage from the full text below while the children just listen. Give the children the first word and ask them to write it in the first space. Check that each child has understood what to do and has written the word in the first space. Continue reading the passage for the second time, stopping at each missing word to allow time for the word to be written by the children in a space on their page. Repeat the words as often as seems necessary.

"Tom will be here <u>soon</u>," Mum called.
"I <u>like</u> to <u>play</u> by myself," Pete said. "I <u>have</u> made an aeroplane."
"I can <u>see</u> that," said Mum. "But be careful <u>you</u> don't <u>get</u> run <u>over</u>."

Name _____   Date _____

These questions are about Pete and the Stick.

Tick the right box.

1 What was the boy's name?

Tom ☐   Ben ☐   Pete ☐   Mark ☐

2 What was he carrying?

a bag ☐   a book ☐   a ball ☐   a stick ☐

3 What size was the stick?

tiny ☐   quite small ☐   short ☐   very, very big ☐

4 Who was walking along with Pete?

a dog ☐   a girl ☐   his shadow ☐   his friend ☐

5 What did Pete pretend he was?

a stick ☐   a tree ☐   an aeroplane ☐   a car ☐

Write a sentence to answer these questions.

6 Why did people get cross?

_____

7 Why didn't Pete notice the people getting cross?

_____

Name _____ **Date** _____

Term 1 Assessment of Progress: Writing

Pretending

- Have you ever pretended to be someone or something?
- Write some words about what you did.

_____
_____

- Write some sentences about what happened. Where you were, what you did and who played with you.

_____
_____
_____
_____
_____
_____
_____
_____
_____
_____

On Target English © Hilary Frost 2001

Term 1 Assessment of Progress: Spelling

   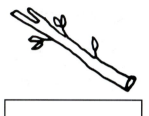

"Tom will be here _____," Mum called.

"I _____ to _____ by myself," Pete said.

"I _____ made an aeroplane."

"I can _____ that," said Mum. "But be careful

_____ don't _____ run _____."

Term 2 Key Concepts: Units 8–14

Text level

Fiction – narrative

- **settings**
Help the children towards an understanding that most of the stories that they write will have a setting, i.e. a place and a time when the events occur. Discuss the settings of stories that are familiar (e.g. traditional) or that have been read recently. Compare the settings of different stories. Consider how the settings influence the events in the story and the behaviour of the key characters. Consider how other, different story themes might be constructed using the same setting.

- **characters**
Identify, list and describe characters from stories currently being read. Discuss and describe them, picking out key words and phrases from the text. Use these words and phrases to write character profiles. The children will begin to express opinions about the characters, stating whether they like them, and why.

Poetry

- **inventing own lines**
It is always extremely difficult for children to feel confident about writing poetry at this age, but one route worth pursuing is by using simple, short poems as models and then beginning to substitute words and lines. Eventually this can be extended to the point where some children might even begin to add their own verses.

Non-fiction

- **alphabetically ordered texts**
Alphabetical ordering is manifestly a crucial skill for referring to dictionaries, glossaries, thesauri and many reference books, so the sooner it is mastered the better. Some will grasp the principles quickly; others will take a little longer. Use opportunities whenever they offer themselves to consider how words can be sorted alphabetically, beginning with single letter ordering, and once this is grasped extending to looking at second or even third letter sorting. OTE assumes some children will have difficulty and need 'refresher' sessions, but the sooner the skills are secured the sooner dictionaries and other reference tools can be used in a meaningful way.

- **diagrams**
In this section of the book flow charts and cyclical diagrams are featured. As with the diagrams covered earlier, demonstrate how carefully drawn diagrams and other illustrations can be a more effective way than simple descriptive prose to convey information.

Sentence level

Grammar

- **agreement**
Many children have the 'handicap' of hearing non-standard English spoken at home and in their wider social circle. This is most frequently characterised by the non-agreement of nouns/pronouns and verbs, e.g. *We was waiting for a bus*. The best and most effective way to help improve their grasp of standard English (*is/are*; *was/were*) is to raise awareness of the issue by having frequent and regular one-minute oral sessions in which all of the class has to try to spot and then indicate (by a show of hands) when the teacher has made a deliberate mistake. With agreement, hearing needs to come before writing.

- **verb tense**
Similarly, oral work on forming past tenses of verbs is critically important. Ensure that the children understand that some simply take a *d* or *ed*, but others are irregular, and frequently the vowel letter is changed, e.g. *run*, *ran*; *sit*, *sat*. But also note that some are more radically altered, e.g. *catch*, *caught*; *go*, *went*.

Sentence construction and punctuation

- **identifying speech**
When opportunities lend themselves, pick out from stories 'the words actually spoken' by a character, and note that these words are contained within speech marks. Compare this with speech bubbles in pictures and comics.

- **commas in lists**
Most children find this an easy skill to develop, but some slip up by including a comma before the final 'and' or 'or' in a sentence containing a list.

- **simple sentences**
Remain constantly vigilant for the correct use of capital letters, both at the beginning of sentences and for the initial letter in proper nouns and in titles. Also, keep alert to any child who is not writing in sentences that are complete, which make sense in their own right.

Word level

Phonics, graphic knowledge and spelling

• common letter strings
As noted previously, teaching and learning some of the common letter strings is important. Continue to collect and display charts that list letter strings, and whenever a new word is encountered during class or group work ensure it is added to the chart on the wall – giving an opportunity to revisit those already in the list.

• vowel phonemes
Particular attention should be given to the teaching and/or consolidation of the vowel phonemes. Some are covered in the following units, but space does not permit a complete coverage. Where the same phoneme (sound) can be represented by different graphemes (letter groups), e.g. *oa*, *oe*, *ow*, then each is taught and practised separately before being brought together.

• compound words
Compound words are an easy way of demonstrating how some words have constituent parts. Also, by being able to analyse words in this way improves the possibilities for better spelling.

• prefixes
Prefixes are frequently associated with the forming of antonyms, and these are the ones focused on in the coming units.

Vocabulary extension

• antonyms
Antonyms are opposites. As well as antonyms formed by the addition of a prefix (see above) there are many others, and these are practised. Also, the children might spot that some words can have more than one antonym, e.g. end: begin, start, commence; or because of homophones: right/wrong, right/left.

Handwriting

• joins
Having been developing letter forms that lend themselves to joining, we now need to begin to encourage the children to actually join the letters in words. To this end the main joins are covered in this book, with these units focusing on horizontal joins to letters without ascenders. Whenever possible, the handwriting patterns are linked to the teaching of letter strings which will be helpful with spelling.

Unit 8 The Castle Rescue

Curriculum references

England (Year 2 Term 2)
Range: Traditional stories, stories from other cultures
Objectives:

> **Text level work**
> 4 to predict story endings/incidents, e.g. from unfinished extracts, while reading with the teacher
> 5 to discuss story settings: to compare differences; to consider how different settings influence events and behaviour
> 13 to use story settings from reading, e.g. redescribe, use in own writing, write a different story in the same setting

> **Sentence level work**
> 5 to use verb tenses with increasing accuracy ...
> 9 to secure the use of simple sentences in own writing

> **Word level work**
> 1 to secure the ... spelling of long vowel phonemes
> 4 to split familiar oral and compound words into their component parts
> 14 to use and practise the four basic handwriting joins:
> • horizontal joins to letters without ascenders

Wales
Range – Pupils should be given opportunities to:
3 write in response to a variety of stimuli, including stories
4 write in a range of forms, incorporating some of the characteristics of those forms; the range should include a variety of narratives, e.g. stories
Skills
1 write with confidence, fluency and accuracy
2 learn about the different purposes and functions of written language
7 punctuate:
• punctuate their writing, be consistent in their use of capital letters
8 spell:
• use their knowledge of sound–symbol relationships and phonological patterns
• write common letter strings with familiar and common words
• spell commonly occurring simple words
9 develop their handwriting:
• build on their knowledge of letter formation to join letters in words

Scotland (AT/PoS Level A/B)
Imaginative writing – Write a brief imaginative story, with discernible organisation and using adequate vocabulary.
Punctuation and structure – Use capital letters and full stops correctly.

Spelling – Spell frequently used words accurately ... The learning of spelling rules should support this.
Handwriting – Form letters and space words legibly in linked script.
Knowledge about language – Understand and use the terms: letter, word, capital, full stop, sentence.

Northern Ireland
Purpose – develop imagination; narrate; describe
Range – stories; simple records of observations; descriptions of people or places
Expected outcomes:
• use the conventional ways of forming letter shapes in upper and lower case
• spell recognisably a range of familiar and important words
• use basic punctuation conventions, including capital letters

On Target English

Interactive Big Book
- The picture can be used to stimulate discussion about the possible outcomes, discovering that various scenarios might offer themselves.
- Use the opportunity to revise the notion of a verb as an action (or doing) word. Ask the children to identify actions and list on the board the corresponding verbs.

Comprehension and Writing Skills
To the rescue
The cloze passage requires literal responses to the picture.
A brave prince
Before beginning to complete the sentences required in this exercise, spend some time considering how sentences can be made more interesting by thinking about and using appropriate verbs and adjectives – not just the first ones that come to mind, e.g. The brave, young prince battled through the thick, dark wood. rather than The prince rode through the wood.
The burning castle
Settings are a fundamental part of stories and storytelling. Consider several well-known traditional stories, and encourage selected volunteers to give their oral descriptions of settings such as the three bears' house, or the giant's home above the clouds from Jack and the Beanstalk. Use Copymaster 1 to support the planning of such a story, which might be written later.
Finish the story
Discuss the possible endings to the story. The group may all wish to write the same ending, but if some children wish to work independently to complete their own versions this should be encouraged and praised. At this stage confidence building is an important role of the teacher.

Teacher's Resource Book 2

Unit 8

ANSWERS

Comprehension
To the rescue
The prince was on a horse.
He was trying to help the princess.
He could not go over the bridge because it was broken.
He went through the thick, dark wood.
A brave prince
individual answers

Sentence and Word Skills
Doing words
Verbs are taught here as 'doing' words in preparation for work in the coming units on tenses etc. The children might spot that very often doing words (or 'verbs', if the teacher judges the group ready to use the term) end in ing or ed.
Capital letters in special naming words
A further opportunity to practise when to use capital letters. Copymaster 2 from this unit revises many of the proper nouns a child will encounter.
o-e words
One of the important long vowel phonemes.
Word sums
This further work on compound words (see also Unit 5) helps the children to discover that words often have component parts, even though not usually as immediately apparent as is the case with compound words.

ANSWERS

Sentence work
Doing words
1 jumping climbing fighting
   falling throwing carrying
2 individual answers
Capital letters in special naming words
1 Prince Ismail Calcutta Queen Anita India
2 Prince Ismail lived in India.
   Princess Roshan lived near a city called Calcutta.
   One day Prince Ismail went to visit Calcutta.

Word work
o-e words
1 smoke globe throne
   robe stone choke
2 smoke rhymes with choke
   robe rhymes with globe
   stone rhymes with throne
Word sums
football toothbrush snowman lunchtime

Homework suggestions
- Write some sentences to describe the setting for the story of The Three Bears.
- Point out that o-e is an awkward letter pattern as it sometimes doesn't sound as it should, e.g. come, gone. Ask the children to look through a book or magazine and find other o-e words, sorting them into two lists – those that behave correctly, and those that don't!

Year 2 Unit 8 Copymaster 1

Name _____ **Date** _____

Story Settings

I am going to write a story about: _____
_____
_____

My story will take place at: _____
_____
_____

A picture of where my story happens:

Some words I will use about where and when my story happens:

_____   _____
_____   _____
_____   _____
_____   _____
_____   _____

Objective: To consider and plan story settings

On Target English © Hilary Frost 2001

Year 2 Unit 8 Copymaster 2

Name _____ **Date** _____

My Personal Record

My name _____

My pet's name _____

My two best friends _____
_____

I live at _____
_____
_____

My birthday _____

My school _____

My school's address _____
_____

My teacher _____

This is my picture:

Objective: To use capital letters for proper nouns

On Target English © Hilary Frost 2001

Unit 9 — Sam's Dictionary

Curriculum references

England (Year 2 Term 2)
Range: Dictionaries
Objectives:

> **Text level work**
> 16 to use dictionaries ... to locate words by using initial letter
> 17 that dictionaries ... give definitions and explanations
> 20 to make class dictionaries ... of special interest words, giving explanations and definitions

> **Sentence level work**
> 8 to use commas to separate items in a list
> 9 to secure the use of simple sentences in own writing

> **Word level work**
> 1 to secure the ... spelling of long vowel phonemes
> 14 to use and practise the four basic handwriting joins:
> • horizontal joins to letters without ascenders

Wales
Range – Pupils should be given opportunities to:
4 write in a range of forms, incorporating some of the characteristics of those forms; the range should include notes, e.g. lists
7 make choices about vocabulary and organise ... factual writing in different ways, e.g. a list
Skills
1 write with confidence, fluency and accuracy
2 ... learn about the different purposes and functions of written language
3 to recognise the alphabetic nature of writing
8 spell:
• use their knowledge of sound–symbol relationships and phonological patterns
• recognise and use simple spelling patterns
• write common letter strings with familiar and common words
9 develop their handwriting:
• build on their knowledge of letter formation to join letters in words

Scotland (AT/PoS Level A/B)
Functional writing – Write briefly in an appropriate form for a variety of practical purposes.
Spelling – Spell frequently used words accurately through using a simple wordbank or dictionary.
Handwriting – Form letters and space words legibly in linked script.
Knowledge about language – Understand and use the terms: letter, word.

Northern Ireland
Purpose express their thoughts and feelings; develop their imagination; narrate; describe; inform and explain; report; record findings
Range – simple records of observations; lists
Expected outcomes:
• make use of names and order of the letters of the alphabet
• spell recognisably a range of familiar and important words

On Target English

Interactive Big Book
- Consider with the children why arranging words in alphabetical order is so important. Show a telephone directory and discuss what a problem it would be if you needed to find a person's telephone number and yet all the names were arranged randomly. Then consider the same for a simple dictionary.
- Discuss the uses of a dictionary, with particular reference to definitions and support for spelling.
- Ask children to look at the ten animals illustrated. Encourage them to list the names which can be written on the board. Help children to put the animals into alphabetical order. Then encourage children to think of animals for the other letters in the alphabet.

Comprehension and Writing Skills
Sam's dictionary
The cloze passage requires literal responses to the page from the animal dictionary.
Spot the mistake
The activity is designed to encourage the children to think about their writing, and where necessary to correct it.
Making a dictionary
Consider how difficult it can be to write definitions of words by asking volunteers to describe something familiar, but without using the actual word. The rest of the group should try to guess what is being defined, e.g. a chair, a donkey (both have four legs and can be sat upon). Use this activity as the basis for beginning to create some class 'topic' dictionaries. Copymaster 1 from this unit will support this.
Animal quiz
Extend, if appropriate, by giving the children other creatures for which they should write short, pithy definitions.

Unit 9

ANSWERS

Comprehension
Sam's dictionary
Sam's dictionary is about animals.
It tells us what each word means.
The first animal is an ant.
After the cat the next animal is a donkey.
Spot the mistake
An ant is a very small animal that lives in big groups.
A bear is a heavy animal that likes to live in a cave.
A cat is a small animal that can live at home with us.
A donkey looks like a small horse with longer ears.

Sentence and Word Skills
Nouns and verbs
As the children are expected to use the correct terminology, it is suggested that if you haven't done so already, you use this opportunity to begin to familiarise the class with 'noun' and 'verb'.
Writing lists
This is a concept that most children find relatively easy to grasp, though some take a while to remember that the last two items are separated by 'and' rather than a comma.
oa, oe and ow words
An opportunity to revisit this important set of vowel digraphs which can represent the same long vowel phoneme. Use copymaster 2 from this unit to support as required.
Alphabetical order
A further opportunity for the children to work on alphabetical ordering by the first letter.

ANSWERS

Sentence work
Nouns and verbs
1. ant climbs
   bear hunts
   cat purrs
   donkey brays
   elephant trumpets
   fox howls
2. Individual answers, e.g.
   dog barks
   bird flies
   fish swims
   snake hisses
   rabbit digs

Writing lists
Sam has drawn monkeys, snakes, hippos, tigers, lions and giraffes.
Miss Drew asked Tom, Gemma, Sophie, Ajit and Wes to help her.
At the zoo we drew pictures of camels, chimps, emus and penguins.

Word work
oa, oe and ow words
Sam has a minnow in his jar.
A doe is a deer.
The goat has two horns.
We found a fat brown toad under the log.
A crow is bigger than a blackbird.
Alphabetical order
alligator camel goat kangaroo lion monkey rabbit squirrel

Homework suggestions
- Collect an animal for each letter of the alphabet, or as many as they can!
- Write definitions for an appropriate number of the animals.

Year 2 Unit 9 Copymaster 1

Name _____ **Date** _____

Making a Dictionary

My dictionary is about _____

Word	Picture	Meaning
_____	☐	_____
_____	☐	_____
_____	☐	_____
_____	☐	_____
_____	☐	_____
_____	☐	_____

Objective: To make a dictionary

On Target English © Hilary Frost 2001

Year 2 Unit 9 Copymaster 2

Name _____ Date _____

oa, *o-e* and *ow* words

Sort the words in the box by their spelling pattern.

| throne blow toast mow nose |
| close float throw grow low |
| boat coat bone goat poke |

o-e words   *oa* words   *ow* words
_____   _____   _____
_____   _____   _____
_____   _____   _____
_____   _____   _____
_____   _____   _____

Write a word to answer each clue:

Cooked bread _____   Part of your face _____

To cut grass _____   An animal with horns _____

Opposite of 'open' _____   Opposite of 'sink' _____

Floats on water _____   Special seat _____

Objective: To spell words with *oa*, *o-e* and *ow*

On Target English © Hilary Frost 2001

Unit 10 Three Billy Goats Gruff

Curriculum references

England (Year 2 Term 2)
Range: Dictionaries
Objectives:

> **Text level work**
> 4 to predict story endings/incidents, e.g. from unfinished extracts, while reading with the teacher
> 5 to discuss story settings: to compare differences; to consider how different settings influence events and behaviour
> 13 to use story settings from reading, e.g. redescribe, use in own writing, write a different story in the same setting

> **Sentence level work**
> 5 to use verb tenses with increasing accuracy in speaking and writing, and to use past tense consistently for narration
> 7 to investigate a range of ... ways of presenting texts, e.g. speech bubbles
> 9 to secure the use of simple sentences in own writing

> **Word level work**
> 7 to use word endings, e.g. ing, to support their reading and spelling
> 14 to use and practise the four basic handwriting joins:
> • horizontal joins to letters without ascenders

Wales
Range – Pupils should be given opportunities to:
3 write in response to a variety of stimuli, including stories
4 write in a range of forms, incorporating some of the characteristics of those forms; the range should include a variety of narratives, e.g. stories
Skills
1 write with confidence, fluency and accuracy
2 ... learn about the different purposes and functions of written language
8 spell:
• recognise and use simple spelling patterns
• spell words with common ... suffixes
9 develop their handwriting:
• build on their knowledge of letter formation to join letters in words

Scotland (AT/PoS Level A/B)
Imaginative writing – Write a brief imaginative story, with discernible organisation and using adequate vocabulary.
Spelling – Spell frequently used words accurately ... The learning of spelling rules should support this.
Handwriting – Form letters and space words legibly in linked script.

Northern Ireland
Purpose – develop imagination; narrate; describe
Range – stories; descriptions of people or places
Expected outcomes:
• spell recognisably a range of familiar and important words
• write correctly structured sentences

On Target English

Interactive Big Book
- When sharing the text and picture focus particularly on the setting. Write words on the board that the children might use later when writing another story using this setting.
- Also, discuss the speech bubbles. Invite speculation as to what each of the characters might have been saying.

Comprehension and Writing Skills
In the country
The children need to interpret the text and select the 'correct' sentences. Ensure, when copying the correct sentences, that capital letters and full stops are used where appropriate.
All about the Billy Goats
This task is similar to the above, but the children are required to choose a 'correct' sentence from a range of optional endings.
Winter fun
The purpose of this task is to encourage the children to develop the concept of 'setting'. Through discussion, and possibly other techniques such as making pictures, the setting should become sufficiently real for the children to write other episodes or other stories based in the same setting. As extra support where appropriate, copymaster 1 from this unit structures the task more tightly.
The sad troll
This parallel activity to the one above is to help the children empathise with the characters in the setting/story.

ANSWERS

Comprehension
In the country
It is a bright, sunny day.
The ducks are on the river.
There is a wood near the field.
There is a horse in the next field.
All about the Billy Goats
The Billy Goats Gruff lived in a field.
They liked to go up the hill.
They liked to eat juicy, green grass.
Under the bridge lived a troll.

Teacher's Resource Book 2

Unit 10

Sentence and Word Skills
Now and then
This provides another opportunity to talk about verbs as action or doing words. It is also intended to introduce the notion of tenses, or time. By looking at verbs we can establish when the action has occurred or will occur – now, in the past or in the future. Previously we considered adding ing, the suffix most normally associated with present tenses, and in this unit we consider how past tense verbs are most often created – by the addition of ed or d (for verbs that end in e). As ever, lots of group work and sharing of examples will help establish the idea, and help children have an understanding that ed is a standard word ending, even if they are tempted to spell it with a final 't', e.g. jumped, not jumpt!

Speech bubbles
This material is a prelude to helping the children understand and begin to write dialogue, which requires them to be able to distinguish the words actually spoken in a dialogue sentence, and to be able to determine who actually spoke the words.

th words
This group includes some of the most frequently used words, so time spent ensuring the children are fully conversant with, and able to spell, these words is time well spent.

Adding ing
A chance to revisit and consolidate the ing suffix, and reinforce the earlier work in the unit related to tenses. Use copymaster 2 from this unit to support as appropriate.

Homework suggestions
- Draw a picture with speech bubbles depicting a recent event involving the child.
- Give an appropriate number/selection of 'th' words for the child to learn.
- Make a list of verbs to which ing or ed can be added.

ANSWERS

Sentence work
Now and then
The troll lived under the bridge.
He liked to eat goats.
He climbed a tree.
The troll sat and watched the goats.
When he saw them coming he jumped out.

Speech bubbles
1. Little Billy Goat Gruff
   Big Billy Goat Gruff
2. I am very hungry.
   I am hungry, too.
3. individual answers

Word work
th words
three thin thank thump think moth teeth cloth

Adding ing
1. thinking eating sleeping helping falling
2. The goats are standing in a field.
   The goats are walking to the bridge.
   The goats are crossing the bridge.
   The troll is shouting at the goats.
   The goats are eating the green grass.

Winter Fun

Write a sentence for each picture to make a story.

_____
_____

_____
_____

_____
_____

_____
_____

Objective: To develop the concept of 'setting'

What Are They Doing?

Finish the sentences.

 He is _____.

 The girl is _____.

 The dog is _____.

 It is _____.

Write a sentence for each picture.

 _____.

 _____.

 _____.

Objective: To use verbs for actions

Unit 11 The Little Sister's Tale

Curriculum references

England (Year 2 Term 2)
Range: Story
Objectives:

> **Text level work**
> 6 to identify and describe characters, expressing own views and using words and phrases from texts
> 14 to write character profiles, e.g. simple descriptions, posters, passports, using key words and phrases that describe or are spoken by the characters in the text

> **Sentence level work**
> 5 to use verb tenses with increasing accuracy in speaking and writing, and to use past tense consistently for narration
> 9 to secure the use of simple sentences in own writing

> **Word level work**
> 4 to investigate and classify words with the same sounds but different spellings
> 7 to use word endings, e.g. ing, to support their reading and spelling
> 14 to use and practise the four basic handwriting joins:
> • horizontal joins to letters without ascenders

Wales
Range – Pupils should be given opportunities to:
3 write in response to a variety of stimuli, including stories
4 write in a range of forms, incorporating some of the characteristics of those forms; the range should include a variety of narratives, e.g. stories, notes, e.g. captions
7 make choices about vocabulary and organise imaginative and factual writing in different ways
Skills
4 write independently on subjects that are of interest to them
5 identify the purpose for which they write
7 punctuate:
• recognise that punctuation is essential to help a reader understand what is written
• punctuate their writing, be consistent in their use of capital letters, full stops
8 spell:
• use their knowledge of sound–symbol relationships and phonological patterns
• recognise and use simple spelling patterns
• write common letter strings with familiar and common words
• spell commonly occurring simple words
• spell words with common suffixes
9 develop their handwriting:
• build on their knowledge of letter formation to join letters in words
Language development – Pupils should be given opportunities to:
3 develop their interest in words and their meanings, and extend their vocabulary through consideration ... of opposites

Scotland (AT/PoS Level A/B)
Functional writing – Write briefly in an appropriate form for a variety of practical purposes.
Imaginative writing – Write a brief imaginative story or poem or dialogue, with discernible organisation and using adequate vocabulary.
Punctuation and structure – Use capital letters and full stops correctly.
Spelling – Spell frequently used words accurately through using a simple wordbank or dictionary.
Handwriting – Form letters and space words legibly in linked script.
Knowledge about language – Understand and use the terms: capital, full stop.

Northern Ireland
Purpose – narrate; describe
Range – labels; captions; stories
Expected outcomes:
• use the conventional ways of forming letter shapes in upper and lower case
• spell recognisably a range of familiar and important words
• use basic punctuation conventions, including capital letters, full stops

On Target English

Interactive Big Book
• Through discussion help the children to suggest words and phrases that might be used to describe the main characters from the extract, and list these on the board.
• The pictures have also been drawn to enable the teacher to introduce discussion of action verbs and of opposites.

Comprehension and Writing Skills
Annie
The exercise supports the children in writing sentences to give literal answers to the questions about Annie.
Annie's family
The notion of organising information drawn from the passage into a table will need considerable support for some children.
Me
In Unit 8 the children prepared a personal record (as a means of learning about the capitalisation of proper

nouns). This, and the following activity, takes this further by listing and describing other attributes of a more subjective kind.

More about me
Help the children not only to consider things they like and dislike, but also to try to consider their reasons. Apply the same approach to other people, using copymaster 1 from this unit to support where necessary.

ANSWERS

Comprehension
Annie
The name of the child is Annie (or Anastasia).
Her hair sticks out like pasta spirals.
Annie is teased by her brother Tom.
The youngest child is Annie (or Anastasia).

Annie's family

Annie	Tom	Kate
hair that sticks out the youngest child does not like her hair	has fluffy curls likes to tell silly jokes	long straight hair

Sentence and Word Skills
Now and then
This unit provides the opportunity to revisit present and past tenses (which take the suffixes ing and ed) and consider them alongside each other. Copymaster 2 from this unit gives the opportunity for the children to consider the changing of tense of whole sentences, noticing how important the verb is to this. Some children will be ready to extend on to verbs that have irregular tenses, e.g. run, ran; catch, caught.

Capital letters and full stops
Introduce this work by writing on the board a short sentence with the capitals, punctuation and word spaces omitted. Ask the children why it is difficult to read, and from this establish the importance of appropriate spacing, punctuation etc.

ee and ea words
Remind the children that ea can represent different sounds, as in meat, head, wear, ear. However, in this activity we are concentrating on ea as in meat, its basic long vowel form. Discuss what other letter groups make a similar sound, i.e. ee. As an extension for some children, it might be worth introducing the concept of whole words that sound the same, but are spelt differently and have different meanings (homonyms), e.g. meat, meet; leak, leek; weak, week; tea, tee; sea, see.

Opposites
Not all the children may be ready, but the term 'antonym' (meaning 'opposite') should be introduced

if possible. A number of opposites are included in the exercise, but it is suggested that a class collection might be started, with new pairs being added whenever children spot them. As an extension, some children will find it interesting to find some words have more than one antonym, sometimes due to a range of meanings, e.g. open – closed/shut; right – wrong/left.

ANSWERS

Sentence work
Now and then

1

Is happening now	Has happened in the past
jumping	jumped
walking	walked
licking	licked
sucking	sucked
kicking	kicked
yelling	yelled

2 has happened in the past
   is happening now
   has happened in the past
   is happening now

3 individual answers

Capital letters and full stops
Her hair is sticking out.
Tom is saying unkind things.
I wish I had curly hair.
My sister Kate has straight hair.

Word work
ee and ea words
Scream rhymes with team
Tree rhymes with bee
Sleep rhymes with sheep
Tea rhymes with sea
Cream rhymes with stream
Sheet rhymes with feet
Week rhymes with leek

Opposites
out – in
no – yes
down – up
best – worst
before – after
dry – wet
open – shut

Homework suggestions
- Make a table (or use copymaster 1 from this unit) to list characteristics of people (friends, relatives, neighbours, TV personalities) that they know.
- Collect pairs of antonyms (suggest an appropriate number) for the class collection.

Year 2 Unit 11 Copymaster 1

Name _____ **Date** _____

People I Know

Name _____ Name _____

Picture	Picture

Name: _____ Name: _____

Words to describe this person: Words to describe this person:
_____ _____
_____ _____
_____ _____
_____ _____

Likes: Likes:
_____ _____
_____ _____

Dislikes: Dislikes:
_____ _____
_____ _____

Objective: To describe people

On Target English © Hilary Frost 2001

What Did They Do?

Underline the verb in each of these sentences.
Write each sentence as if it happened last week.

 They play with their friends.
_____

 They visit their grandparents.
_____

 We climb the tree.
_____

 She paints the door.
_____

 I bath my dog.
_____

 I talk to my uncle.
_____

Objective: To write sentences in the past tense

Unit 12 In Daisy's Secret Drawer

Curriculum references

England (Year 2 Term 2)
Range: Poem with predictable language
Objectives:

> **Text level work**
> 9 to identify and discuss patterns of rhythm, rhyme and other features of sound in different poems
> 10 to comment on and recognise when the reading aloud of a poem makes sense and is effective
> 11 to identify and discuss favourite poems and poets, using appropriate terms (poet, poem, verse, rhyme, etc.) and referring to the language of the poem
> 15 to use structures from poems as a basis for writing, by extending or substituting elements, inventing own lines, verses; to make class collections, illustrate with captions; to write own poems from initial jottings and words

> **Sentence level work**
> 4 to be aware of the need for grammatical agreement in speech and writing, matching verbs to nouns/pronouns correctly
> 8 to use commas to separate items in a list
> 9 to secure the use of simple sentences in own writing

> **Word level work**
> 14 to use and practise the four basic handwriting joins:
> • horizontal joins to letters without ascenders

Wales
Range – Pupils should be given opportunities to:
3 write in response to a variety of stimuli, including poems
4 write in a range of forms, incorporating some of the characteristics of those forms; the range should include poems
7 make choices about vocabulary and organise imaginative and factual writing in different ways, e.g. a cumulative pattern in a poem
Skills
2 ... learn about the different purposes and functions of written language
5 identify the purpose for which they write
7 punctuate:
• recognise that punctuation is essential to help a reader understand what is written
• punctuate their writing, be consistent in their use of capital letters, full stops and ... begin to use commas
8 spell:
• use their knowledge of sound–symbol relationships and phonological patterns

- recognise and use simple spelling patterns
- write common letter strings with familiar and common words
- spell commonly occurring simple words
9 develop their handwriting:
- build on their knowledge of letter formation to join letters in words

Scotland (AT/PoS Level A/B)
Imaginative writing – Write a brief imaginative poem, with discernible organisation and using adequate vocabulary.
Punctuation and structure – Use capital letters and full stops correctly.
Spelling – Spell frequently used words accurately through using a simple wordbank or dictionary. The learning of spelling rules should support this.
Handwriting – Form letters and space words legibly in linked script.
Knowledge about language – Understand and use the terms: letter, word, capital, full stop, sentence, drafting, redrafting.

Northern Ireland
Purpose – express thoughts and feelings; develop imagination; narrate; describe
Range – poems
Expected outcomes:
- spell recognisably a range of familiar and important words
- use basic punctuation conventions, including capital letters, full stops
- write correctly structured sentences

On Target English

Interactive Big Book
- Share the poem, reading it together and in 'rounds'. If possible find other number and counting rhymes, songs and poems, e.g. One, two buckle my shoe, Ten green bottles, The twelve days of Christmas.
- How many objects beginning with 'ch' can the children find in the drawer? List these on the board, adding others in a second list.

Comprehension and Writing Skills
Daisy's drawer
The children need to match the correct answers to four questions. Ensure the children are thinking about the use of capital letters and punctuation as they do this.
Daisy
Here the children need to consider how the poem can help them with the information to complete the sentences, but it is suggested that this activity should

Teacher's Resource Book 2

Unit 12

be undertaken orally before the children attempt to undertake it independently.

Your secret drawer
It might take some careful teaching to get some children to the point where they can begin to work on a poem like the one suggested, but with support most children will find great satisfaction once it has been done.

A special copy
Copymaster frame 1 from this unit might be used to support the work, or as an incentive for children to collect other 'favourite poems' for the class anthology.

ANSWERS

Comprehension
Daisy's drawer
1 There were four hair grips in Daisy's drawer.
2 She could write with the felt tip pens.
3 The string was chewed-up.
4 She had ten bags of crisps.

Daisy
Daisy liked to hide things in her secret drawer.
Daisy liked playing pop songs on her cassette.
Daisy liked to eat oranges and crisps.
Daisy had three love letters.

Sentence and Word Skills
Using is and are
The best way to teach agreement is orally; indeed most errors occur when children have acquired erroneous usage from their family or peers, so undertake frequent sessions in which you offer a sentence, using 'is' or 'are' correctly or incorrectly, with the children all raising their hands whenever you 'get it wrong'. The additional part to the 'rule' is that when referring to I, neither is nor are is used, but am.

Using commas and full stops
Another important opportunity to secure the punctuation of lists and sentences.

ch words
As with sh and th, ch is an important consonant digraph for the children to feel comfortable with and confident is using when trying to spell unfamiliar words. Notice how often ch is preceded by t when it appears at the end of a word. Copymaster 2 from this unit provides additional practice.

Hidden words
A simple, hopefully enjoyable, way to draw the attention of the children to five important words they need, for different reasons, to be able to spell with confidence.

ANSWERS

Sentence work
Using is and are
1 Daisy's secret drawer is beside her bed.
   Lots of things are in the drawer.
   A ribbon is in it.
   Six felt tips are in it.
   Ten bags of crisps are in Daisy's secret drawer.
2 individual answers

Using commas and full stops
1 Mum said Daisy should throw away the paper-clips, string and orange pips.
2 individual answers

Word work
ch words
1 Words starting with ch: chimp, chopsticks, chicks, chips, chest, chess
   Words ending with ch: match, watch, patch, catch

Hidden words
1 catch, chess, match, chick, chest
2 ch

Homework suggestions
- Collect number and counting poems, or other particular favourites. If possible make a collection of counting poems handed down through families or special to the locality.
- Give a selection of ch words to learn to spell.

Year 2 Unit 12 Copymaster 1

Name _____ **Date** _____

My Favourite Poem

Title _____
Poet _____

I like this poem because _____
_____

Objective: To express an opinion

On Target English © Hilary Frost 2001

Year 2 Unit 12 Copymaster 2

Name _____ **Date** _____

ch, th or sh?

	A young chicken	_____ ick
	Antonym of 'fat'	_____ in
	A large boat	_____ ip
	Likes bright lights	mo _____
	We eat breakfast from this	di _____
	For telling the time	wat _____
	Belongs to the monkey family	_____ imp
	Need to clean twice a day	tee _____
	A favourite sport	fi _____ ing
	A type of bird	fin _____
	Midday meal	lun _____
	Tame rabbits live here	hut _____

Objective: To practise *ch*, *th* and *sh* words

On Target English © Hilary Frost 2001

Unit 13 In Hospital

Curriculum references

England (Year 2 Term 2)
Range: Dictionaries
Objectives:

> **Text level work**
> 17 [that dictionaries] ... give definitions and explanations
> 20 to make class dictionaries ... of special interest words, giving explanations and definitions

> **Sentence level work**
> 4   to be aware of grammatical agreement in speech and writing, matching nouns to nouns/pronouns correctly
> 6   to identify speech marks in reading, understand their purpose, use the terms correctly

> **Word level work**
> 1   to secure the ... spelling of long vowel phonemes
> 10 new words from reading linked to particular topics, to build individual collections of personal interest or significant words
> 14 to use and practise the four basic handwriting joins:
> • horizontal joins to letters without ascenders

Wales
Range – Pupils should be given opportunities to:
3   write in response to a variety of stimuli, including stories, poems, classroom activities and personal experience
4   write in a range of forms, incorporating some of the characteristics of those forms; the range should include notes, e.g. lists, captions
7   make choices about vocabulary and organise ... factual writing in different ways
Skills
2   understand the difference between print and pictures, understanding the connections between speech and writing, and learn about the different purposes and functions of written language
3   to recognise the alphabetic nature of writing and discriminate between letters
4   write independently on subjects that are of interest to them
7   punctuate:
• recognise that punctuation is essential to help a reader understand what is written
8   spell:
• use their knowledge of sound–symbol relationships and phonological patterns
• recognise and use simple spelling patterns
• write common letter strings with familiar and common words
9   develop their handwriting:
• build on their knowledge of letter formation to join letters in words
Language development – Pupils should be given opportunities to:
1   consider the vocabulary, grammar and structures of written standard English
3   develop their interest in words and their meanings, and extend their vocabulary

Scotland (AT/PoS Level A/B)
Functional writing – Write briefly in an appropriate form for a variety of practical purposes.
Spelling – Spell frequently used words accurately through using a simple wordbank or dictionary.
Handwriting – Form letters and space words legibly in linked script.

Northern Ireland
Purpose – inform and explain; report
Range – labels; captions; descriptions of people or places
Expected outcomes:
• use the conventional ways of forming letter shapes in upper and lower case
• make use of names and order of the letters of the alphabet
• use basic punctuation conventions
• write correctly structured sentences

On Target English

Interactive Big Book
• Share the text and pictures, identifying as many items as possible that might need definition if the reader had never been to hospital. Consider the function of the glossary. Are there other words that could usefully be added to the glossary? Note how the words are arranged alphabetically.

Comprehension and Writing Skills
Chris goes to hospital
Before beginning this activity the children need to think carefully about the possible responses, especially when the answer is 'can't tell'. Use this copying of sentences exercise as another excuse to encourage correct sentence punctuation.

Using glossaries
In this section the children need to complete their own sentences, the beginnings of each answer being given.

At the dentist
First discuss the sequence of pictures, relating to the children's own experience of visiting their dentist. Write some caption sentences to describe the events in each picture. Finally, write a glossary definition for each word, after which the children might check their

Teacher's Resource Book 2

Unit 13

definitions with those in a simple dictionary. Use copymaster 1 from this unit for support as appropriate.
Healthy teeth
The children need to consider carefully the significance and relative importance of the four statements. As an extension ask the children to consider other things which might help keep teeth healthy.

ANSWERS

Comprehension
Chris goes to hospital
Chris has pains in his leg. (False)
In the hospital Chris went to bed. (True)
The nurse gives Chris some medicine. (True)
Chris has never been in hospital before. (Can't tell)
Using glossaries
This unit is about staying in hospital.
A glossary tells us the meanings of words in a passage.
The word medicine means special drugs that make people well again.
A place where sick people are looked after is called a hospital.

Sentence and Word Skills
Using was and were
As with the previous work on 'is and are', ensure that plenty of work is conducted orally before beginning to consider more formally and in a written context that was relates to a singular noun or pronoun and were to a plural noun or pronoun. Some children will come from situations in which was and were are interchangeable, so it might take a lot of practice before the correct noun/verb agreement 'sounds' right.
Speech marks
As well as discussing the example provided in the teaching box, ask the children to find examples of speech marks in their reading books and elsewhere. Note that the speech marks act as an alternative to speech bubbles in a text (as opposed to pictorial) context.
u-e, ue and ew
Another important set of vowel digraphs that represent the same phoneme. As an extension some children might be asked to find other words with the same sound, but when it is spelt 'oo', as in spoon. Use copymaster 2 from this unit to support this work.
Collecting words
The main purpose of this simple task is to encourage the pupils to take responsibility for collecting their own words in lists or spelling logs, and/or for creating a class dictionary. Some children might be given other useful topics on which to base word collections.

ANSWERS

Sentence work
Using was and were
1   Chris was looking unwell.
    His mum was worried about him.
    There were lots of children in the hospital.
    They were all unwell.
    The nurses were helping them to get better.
2   individual answers
Speech marks
I want to go home.
We will both go home tomorrow.
I hope so.

Word work
u-e, ue and ew
flute tube crew
blue cube screw
clue prune chew
Collecting words
individual answers

Homework suggestion
- Learn the words collected about a hospital or the words about a school.

Name _____ Date _____

At the Dentist

Glossary

Objective: To write captions and glossary definitions

Year 2 Unit 13 Copymaster 2

Name _____ **Date** _____

ew, *u-e*, *oo* words

		t	c	s	b	
	t	u	h	c	l	
c	u	b	e	r	u	b
	n	e	w	e	e	r
d	e	w	f	w		o
		m	o			o
s	p	o	o	n		m
o		o	d			
o		n	J	u	n	e
n	b	l	e	w		

Sort the words hidden in the box into three lists.

ew words	*u-e* words	*oo* words
_____	_____	_____
_____	_____	_____
_____	_____	_____
_____	_____	_____
_____	_____	_____

Objective: To practise *ew*, *u-e* and *oo* words

On Target English © Hilary Frost 2001

Unit 14 Growing a Sunflower

Curriculum references

England (Year 2 Term 2)
Range: Explanations
Objectives:

Text level work
19 to read flow charts and cyclical diagrams that explain a process
21 to produce simple flow charts or diagrams that explain a process

Sentence level work
5 to use verb tenses with increasing accuracy in speaking and writing and to use past tense consistently for narration
9 to secure the use of simple sentences in own writing

Word level work
1 to secure the ... spelling of long vowel phonemes
8 to spell words with common prefixes, e.g. un to indicate the negative
14 to use and practise the four basic handwriting joins:
• horizontal joins to letters without ascenders

Wales
Range – Pupils should be given opportunities to:
3 write in response to a variety of stimuli, including classroom activities and personal experience
4 write in a range of forms, incorporating some of the characteristics of those forms; the range should include records, e.g. observations
Skills
2 understand the difference between print and pictures, understanding the connections between speech and writing, and learn about the different purposes and functions of written language
4 write independently on subjects that are of interest to them
7 punctuate:
• recognise that punctuation is essential to help a reader understand what is written
• punctuate their writing, be consistent in their use of capital letters, full stops and question marks
8 spell:
• use their knowledge of sound–symbol relationships and phonological patterns
• recognise and use simple spelling patterns
• write common letter strings with familiar and common words
• spell commonly occurring simple words
• spell words with common prefixes
9 develop their handwriting:
• build on their knowledge of letter formation to join letters in words

Language development – Pupils should be given opportunities to:
3 develop their interest in words and their meanings, and extend their vocabulary through consideration ... of opposites

Scotland (AT/PoS Level A/B)
Functional writing – Write briefly in an appropriate form for a variety of practical purposes.
Punctuation and structure – Use capital letters and full stops correctly.
Spelling – Spell frequently used words accurately.
Handwriting – Form letters and space words legibly in linked script.
Knowledge about language – Understand and use the terms: capital, full stop, sentence.

Northern Ireland
Purpose – describe; inform and explain; record findings
Range – captions; simple records of observations; diagrams
Expected outcomes:
• use the conventional ways of forming letter shapes in upper and lower case
• spell recognisably a range of familiar and important words
• use basic punctuation conventions, including capital letters, full stops
• write correctly structured sentences

On Target English

Interactive Big Book
🍎 Compare and contrast the two depictions of a sunflower – one the artist's impression, which reflects the sheer glory and beauty of this flower; the other a diagram which helps us to understand more about it. Note that they are very different, but both have their place.

Comprehension and Writing Skills
Watch it grow
The children need to have considered and discussed the sequence of events before being able to correctly order these sentences. Notice how this is an example of a cyclical diagram, in that the process never stops. Compare this with the children with, say, making a sandwich, in which the process has a beginning and a finite conclusion. This, too, can be illustrated as a flow diagram, but as a straight line without the last stage flowing back into the first.
What is happening?
The children need to write short captions for four of the stages. Discuss how captions need to be short and precise.

Birds in spring
Use copymaster 1 from this unit to help frame the children's work, where necessary. For some, the technicality of constructing the diagram can be as tricky as considering the content!

The seasons
Again, the frame on copymaster 1 from this unit might be used for support.

ANSWERS

Comprehension
Watch it grow
The seeds drop from the plant.
The seeds are in the ground.
The roots begin to grow.
The plant has a flower.

What is happening?
individual answers

Sentence and Word Skills
Now and then
Having considered past tenses of verbs that can be formed by the addition of d or ed, this unit gives the opportunity to consider some of the more common irregular past tense forms. Children are often interested to realise that many of the irregular verb forms are created merely by altering the medial vowel, e.g. dig, dug; throw, threw.

Capital letters
Another opportunity to secure the notion of capital letters being required to begin sentences, for 'special' names and for the personal pronoun 'I'.

al words
Often this vowel digraph is taught as 'all', but as can be seen from the words used in the activities (e.g. ball, walk) many words have the sound without the second 'l', so it makes things much clearer for the children, and is technically more accurate, to teach it as 'al'. Also, use the opportunity to revise the ing letter pattern. Copymaster 2 from this unit will support the activity, if required.

Prefixes
Briefly revise opposites (antonyms), asking the children for suggestions of opposites to words you write on the board. Start with a selection where the antonym is a different word, e.g. hot/cold, before moving on to words such as lucky/unlucky, lock/unlock. Discuss how the same letters (un) added as a prefix can have the effect of making the opposite. For a list of such words, refer to a dictionary.

ANSWERS

Sentence work
Now and then
1. Dad gave me some seeds.
   He told me I could plant them near the house.
   We went to get some compost.
   The seeds grew into strong plants.

2.

Is happening now	Has happened in the past
throw	threw
blow	blew
begin	began
feel	felt
see	saw
say	said

Capital letters
Old Mrs Barnard gave me some seeds.
I shared them with Jodie.
Jodie said I was kind.
My brother Ben asked Mrs Barnard if he could have some.

Word work
al words
1. stall wall ball bald call walk talk fall
2. calling talking falling walking

Prefixes
untie   unlucky
unlock   unwell

Homework suggestions
- Make a cyclical diagram of the main events in the child's normal day (24 hours).
- Collect some irregular forms of verb past tenses, learning to spell an appropriate number.
- Collect some 'al' words, for a class collection.

Name _____ **Date** _____

Flow Diagrams

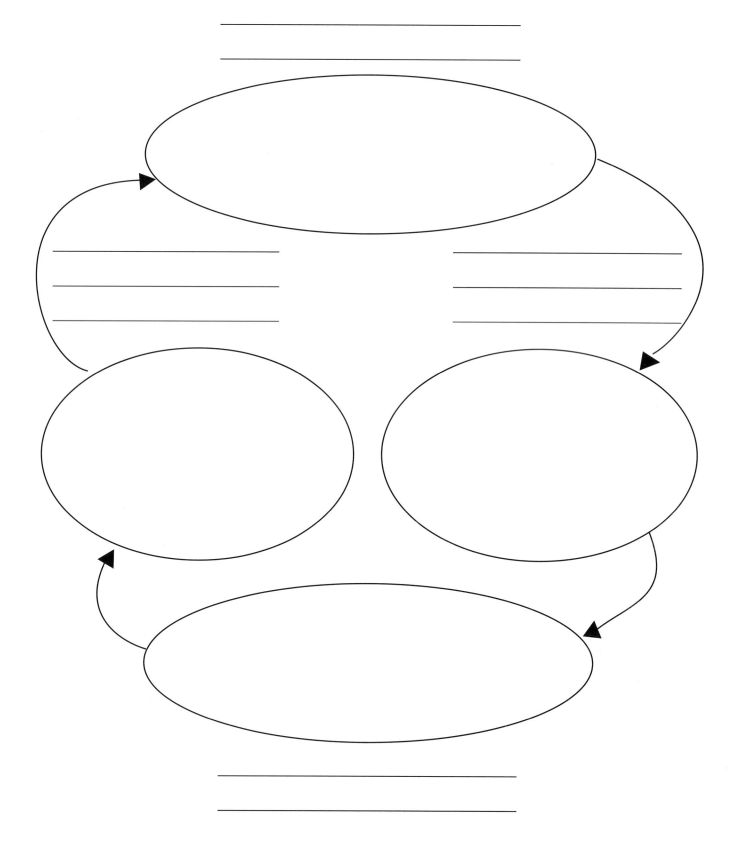

Objective: To construct a flow diagram

al words

Write an *al* word to go with each picture.

_____   _____   _____

_____   _____   _____

Write an *al* word that ends with *ing* to go with each picture.

_____   _____   _____

Objective: To spell words with *al*

Term 2 Assessment of Progress: Comprehension

Name _____ **Date** _____

Term 2 Assessment of Progress: Comprehension

Becoming a Frog

The frog lays her eggs, which are called frogspawn.

The tadpoles grow inside the jelly. It keeps them safe and feeds them.

They hatch and grow two back legs.

The tadpoles breathe through gills. Their tails help them swim.

The tail disappears and they swim with their legs.

The small frog can now leave the water. The tadpole has become a frog.

Teacher's Note for spelling assessment on page 4
First, discuss the large picture and the pictures around it, ensuring the children know what each picture represents. Ask the children to write the name of each small picture in the box underneath it.
Read through the passage from the full text below while the children just listen. Give the children the first word and ask them to write it in the first space. Check that each child has understood what to do and has written the word in the first space. Continue reading the passage for the second time, stopping at each missing word to allow time for the word to be written by the children in a space on their page. Repeat the words as often as necessary.

The <u>three</u> children are <u>looking</u> for frogspawn. They <u>have</u> a pond at <u>home</u>. They <u>want</u> the tadpoles to <u>grow</u> into frogs and <u>live</u> in their <u>garden</u>.

| Name _____ | Date _____ |

These questions are about *Becoming a Frog*.

Tick the right box.

1 What are the frog's eggs called?

jelly ☐   frogspawn ☐   scrambled ☐   frogeggs ☐

2 Where do the tadpoles grow?

in the frog ☐   in the water ☐   in the jelly ☐

3 What does the tadpole breathe through?

mouth ☐   nose ☐   gills ☐   ears ☐

4 What do they use to swim after the tail disappears?

front legs ☐   back legs ☐   tail ☐   body ☐

Write a sentence to answer these questions.

5 Why is the frogspawn jelly important?

_____

6 Which of the tadpole's legs grow first?

_____

7 Do frogs leave the water before or after their tails disappear?

_____

On Target English © Hilary Frost 2001

Name _____ **Date** _____

Term 2 Assessment of Progress: Writing

Growing a Flower

A boy has written about how he grew a flower from a seed.

I planted a seed in the soil. Rain fell on the soil and the sun kept it warm. The plant began to shoot. It became tall and had a big flower. After the flower died, seed pods grew. Seeds fell from the plant.

Make a diagram with captions to show what the boy is describing in his writing.

Term 2 Assessment of Progress: Spelling

The _____ children are _____ for frogspawn. They _____ a pond at _____. They _____ the tadpoles to _____ into frogs and _____ in their _____.

Term 3 Key Concepts: Units 15–20

Text level

Fiction – narrative

• evaluating
Children will be sharing and reading a range of stories and they should begin to be encouraged to express opinions about them. This can be facilitated by looking at two or three books by the same author, discussing them in the terms that the children have previously been taught to consider: theme or plot, setting and characters. Whenever undertaking such an exercise, the children should be helped to formulate reasons for their opinions, rather than simply stating whether or not they enjoyed or liked a book.

Thinking more deeply about their reading and so appreciating the elements of story writing, i.e. narrative/plot, setting, characterisation and dialogue, will spill over into supporting them when beginning to write more sustained stories

• using book covers
Book covers and jackets are devised to tempt and attract the potential reader, but they also provide useful information about the book and the author. Collect several books to share with the class or group, and discuss what can be established about the book, e.g. the title, the author, pictorial clues and blurb describing the content, other books by the same author, what reviewers may have thought of the book etc. Not all books will have the same information, but give titles to volunteer 'detectives' who, without opening the covers, describe as much as they can about the book.

Poetry

• collecting and writing
Continue to make class collections or an anthology of favourite poems, beginning to introduce humour and poems with sound effects, e.g. nonsense poems, tongue twisters, riddles. Some children will enjoy learning some verses, if not complete poems, and performing them to the class.

Also, use some of the children's favourite poems as models for writing, beginning by simply substituting words, and developing by substituting lines until they are able to write additional verses or a completely new poem based on the same structure.

Non-fiction

• fact/fiction
It is often said that many children in the early years of formal schooling are still not immediately distinguishing fact and fantasy, so when approaching the distinction between fact and fiction, the teacher should not underestimate the conceptual leap required by some pupils.

• finding the information
In group sessions, share a range of non-fiction books and discover with the children that there are various important mechanisms for guiding the reader – notably the contents and index. Also, help the children to appreciate that they can skim-read the title, contents, chapter headings and sub-headings to help them home in on the relevant parts of the book for the task in hand.

• non-fiction models
Establish with the children, by sharing a range of texts, that stories and information books are set out differently; the latter often having headings and sub-headings, captions, diagrams etc. However, it is not easy for most children of this age to manipulate headings unless these are effectively the plan of the piece of writing, into which the text/diagrams are placed. In other words, encourage the children to work to the headings, rather than adding headings retrospectively.

Sentence level

Grammar

• agreement
As in the earlier units of this book, remember that the most effective way to help improve their grasp of noun/verb agreement (e.g. I am, he is, they are) is by regular brief oral sessions in which all of the class has to try to spot and then indicate (by a show of hands) when the teacher has made a deliberate mistake. With agreement, hearing needs to come before writing.

• verb tense
Similarly, oral work on forming past tenses of verbs is very important. Remind the children that some simply take a d or ed, while others are irregular, and frequently the vowel letter is changed, e.g. run, ran; sit, sat, or are more radically altered, e.g. catch, caught; go, went.

Sentence construction and punctuation

• commas in lists
Evidence has shown that this is not a difficult concept, though some pupils will need to be reminded that there is no comma between the last two items in a list when 'and' or 'or' are used.

• demarcating sentences

Consolidate the concept of a sentence as a unit of language that makes sense on its own. All sentences begin with a capital letter and, as suggested previously, it can be helpful to suggest that all sentences must end with a full stop. The question mark and exclamation mark can be used in place of a full stop because each of these two punctuation marks has a full stop built into it.

• questions

Work on question sentences and question marks is often best delivered in the context of comparing them with statements, which end with a full stop.

Word level

Phonics, graphic knowledge and spelling

• revision

The children will have progressed at different speeds with regard to phonic awareness and spelling, and this is a time to focus on both general and specific revision, while teaching some of the trickier and confusing phonemes.

• suffixes

The concept of prefixes taught earlier and now the teaching of suffixes can form the basis for developing the concept of word families built from roots with the addition of various prefixes and suffixes.

Vocabulary extension

• synonyms

Raising awareness of synonyms becomes increasingly important as children are encouraged to 'find a better word' when editing and revising their work. It can be linked with work on antonyms (opposites) with some children, but the key is to help pupils towards an enjoyment and satisfaction in broadening their actively used vocabulary.

Handwriting

• joins

Having been developing letter forms that lend themselves to joining, we now need to begin to encourage the children to actually join the letters in words. To this end the main joins are covered in this book, with these units focusing on diagonal joins to letters with ascenders. Whenever possible, the handwriting patterns are linked to the teaching of letter strings which will be helpful with spelling.

Unit 15 Goldilocks

Curriculum references

England (Year 2 Term 3)
Range: Extended stories
Objectives:

Text level work
3 to notice the difference between spoken and written forms through retelling known stories
10 to write sustained stories, using their knowledge of story elements: narrative, settings, characterisation, dialogue and the language of story

Sentence level work
2 ... using simple gender forms correctly
6 to turn statements into questions, learning a range of 'wh' words typically used to open questions and to add question marks

Word level work
1 to secure phonemic spellings from previous five terms
7 to spell words with common suffixes, e.g. -ly
11 to practise handwriting in conjunction with the phonic and spelling patterns (being learnt)
12 to use the four basic handwriting joins:
• diagonal joins to letters with ascenders

Wales
Range – Pupils should be given opportunities to:
3 write in response to a variety of stimuli, including stories
4 write in a range of forms, incorporating some of the characteristics of those forms; the range should include a variety of narratives, e.g. stories
Skills
7 punctuate:
• recognise that punctuation is essential to help a reader understand what is written
• punctuate their writing, be consistent in their use of capital letters, full stops and question marks
8 spell:
• write each letter of the alphabet
• use their knowledge of sound–symbol relationships and phonological patterns
• recognise and use simple spelling patterns
• spell words with common ... suffixes
9 develop their handwriting:
• build on their knowledge of letter formation to join letters in words
Language development – Pupils should be given opportunities to:
1 consider the vocabulary, grammar and structures of written standard English

Scotland (AT/PoS Level A/B)
Imaginative writing – Write a brief imaginative story or poem or dialogue, with discernible organisation and using adequate vocabulary.
Punctuation and structure – Use capital letters and full stops correctly.
Spelling – Spell frequently used words accurately through using a simple wordbank or dictionary. The learning of spelling rules should support this.
Handwriting – Form letters and space words legibly in linked script.

Northern Ireland
Purpose – narrate
Range – stories
Expected outcomes:
• spell recognisably a range of familiar and important words
• use basic punctuation conventions, including capital letters, full stops and question marks
• write correctly structured sentences

On Target English

Interactive Big Book
 Discuss the story, considering, among other things, the narrative, settings, characterisation, dialogue – including what questions the characters might be asking.

Comprehension and Writing Skills
What Goldilocks sees
The children should have discussed the possible answers before being expected to write the sentences required in this activity.
What does she say?
The children need to relate the dialogue to certain stages in the story.
Goldilocks' story
This activity points up the three important story components of character, setting and plot. Copymaster 1 from this unit will provide support.
Better words
Discuss how important it is for writers not to use the first word that occurs to them, but to consider carefully what is the best word to use in a particular context.

Teacher's Resource Book 2

Unit 15

ANSWERS

Comprehension
What Goldilocks sees
Goldilocks sees a pretty little cottage in the wood.
She eats the porridge because she is hungry.
She sleeps on the little bed.
The three bears are cross with Goldilocks.
What does she say?
What a pretty little cottage.
That was good!
I am tired.

Sentence and Word Skills
Girl or boy, man or woman?
Share with the children words that can be used in place of nouns, i.e. pronouns. Demonstrate how repetitive and clumsy sentences would be if we didn't use such words. Invite the children to suggest such words, and list these on the board. Then sort the list into those for males, those used for females and those that can be used either for males or females.
Question words
Make a collection of the 'wh' question words (e.g. Who, Where, When, Why, Which, What) and help the children to learn how to spell them.
a-e words
An opportunity to revise 'magic e' spellings, and in particular to appreciate that recognising rhyming patterns in words can be helpful when learning to spell. Copymaster 2 from this unit provides extra practice.
Suffixes
Adding ly as a suffix changes the root word, often forming an adverb – a word which tells how a verb is carried out. This is something that some children will be able to appreciate, and will help them later when they move on to more formally learn about using adverbs.

ANSWERS

Sentence work
Girl or boy, man or woman?
1 She said it was his porridge.
   She said the bed was hers.
   He (or she) saw her running away.
   She was frightened of him.
2 individual answers

Question words
1 What is your name?
   Where do you live?
   When is your birthday?
   Who ate the Three Bears' porridge?
2 individual answers

Word work
a-e words
individual answers
Suffixes
1 lovely
   smartly
   safely
   lonely
   quietly
   quickly
2 individual answers

Homework suggestions
- Learn to spell all of the wh words collected.
- Collect and learn how to spell two additional a-e words from each rhyming set.

Year 2 Unit 15 Copymaster 1

Name _____ **Date** _____

A Story Plan

This is my plan for a story about _____

In my story I will have:

Name

_____

_____

_____

Description

_____

_____

_____

_____

_____

Where and when the story will happen:
_____
_____

What will happen:
- at the beginning
_____
_____

- in the middle
_____
_____

- at the end
_____
_____

Objective: To write a story plan

On Target English © Hilary Frost 2001

Year 2 Unit 15 Copymaster 2

Name _____ Date _____

a-e words

Write a word from the box under each picture.

| crate   plate   plane   flame   snake   crane   spade   shave |

   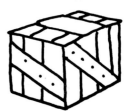

_____ _____ _____ _____

_____ _____ _____ _____

What am I? (All the answers are *a-e* words.)

I have wheels and can be strapped to your foot. s _____
I'm a fruit and grow on a vine. g _____
I'm a strong wind. g _____
I'm what you do after you've been sleeping. w _____
I'm sticky and used to wrap parcels. t _____

Objective: To spell words with *a-e*

On Target English © Hilary Frost 2001

Unit 16 Teeth

Curriculum references

England (Year 2 Term 3)
Range: Extended stories
Objectives:

Text level work
16 to scan a text to find specific sections, e.g. key words or phrases, sub-headings
20 to write non-fiction texts, using texts read as models for own writing, e.g. headings, sub-headings, captions

Sentence level work
3 to use standard form of verbs in speaking and writing
6 to turn statements into questions, learning a range of 'wh' words typically used to open questions ... and to add question marks

Word level work
1 to secure phonemic spellings from previous five terms
10 to use synonyms and other alternative words/phrases that express same or similar meanings
11 to practise handwriting in conjunction with the phonic and spelling patterns (being learnt)
12 to use the four basic handwriting joins:
• diagonal joins to letters with ascenders

Wales
Range – Pupils should be given opportunities to:
4 write in a range of forms, incorporating some of the characteristics of those forms; the range should include ... notes, e.g. lists, captions; records, e.g. observations
Skills
2 learn about the different purposes and functions of written language
4 write independently on subjects that are of interest to them
5 identify the purpose for which they write
7 punctuate:
• recognise that punctuation is essential to help a reader understand what is written
• punctuate their writing, be consistent in their use of capital letters, full stops and question marks
8 spell:
• use their knowledge of sound–symbol relationships and phonological patterns
• recognise and use simple spelling patterns
• write common letter strings with familiar and common words
9 develop their handwriting:
• build on their knowledge of letter formation to join letters in words

Language development – Pupils should be given opportunities to:
1 consider the vocabulary, grammar and structures of written standard English
3 develop their interest in words and their meanings, and extend their vocabulary through consideration ... of words with similar meanings

Scotland (AT/PoS Level A/B)
Functional writing – Write briefly in an appropriate form for a variety of practical purposes.
Punctuation and structure – Use capital letters and full stops correctly.
Spelling – Spell frequently used words accurately.
Handwriting – Form letters and space words legibly in linked script.

Northern Ireland
Purpose – inform and explain; report; record findings
Range – labels; captions; simple records of observations
Expected outcomes:
• use the conventional ways of forming letter shapes in upper and lower case
• spell recognisably a range of familiar and important words
• use basic punctuation conventions, including capital letters, full stops and question marks
• write correctly structured sentences

On Target English

Interactive Big Book
🍎 Use the information passage to demonstrate certain important features of non-fiction writing with which the children need to become familiar, i.e. main headings and sub-headings, simple direct sentences, diagrams supported by captions.
🍎 Use the smaller pictures of the children undertaking certain actions to introduce the section on verbs.

Comprehension and Writing Skills
Using teeth
The children should use properly constructed and punctuated short sentences to answer these literal questions.
Put it right
This task requires the pupils to interrogate the text to establish what is wrong with the facts. Make the point that when reading for information it is important to do so carefully.
Writing information
Some children will feel confident using the model, and they can be encouraged to develop and modify it, whereas others will need support, and for those

Teacher's Resource Book 2

Unit 16

needing a lot of help the writing frame on copymaster 1 from this unit will prove useful.

ANSWERS

Comprehension
Using teeth
Canine teeth are used for tearing food.
Cows chew their food.
A lion tears its food.
A molar tooth is used for chewing food.
Put it right
Lions tear their food.
Hamsters cut their food.
Cows chew their food.

Sentence and Word Skills
Verbs
This section reinforces the notion of a verb and the link between verbs and nouns.
Questions and answers
Ensure there is adequate discussion with oral examples before the children are expected to complete this activity, which is quite sophisticated for some children.
ai and ay words
There are three commonly used words with this spelling pattern which in some regional accents do not conform to their pure phoneme, i.e. said, says and again. Give these words special attention if they are exceptions for your children. Copymaster 2 from this unit has been devised to provide an extension activity, if required, linking the ai and ay words to a-e words as practised in the previous unit.
Words with similar meanings
As was noted earlier, the children should be encouraged to begin to appreciate that their first attempt at a piece of writing can usually be improved and polished. This will start to establish the notions of 'first draft' and 'redrafting'. Initially, the most obvious way in which pupils might be helped to see the need for this is with the selection of 'the best word', which is the purpose for considering synonyms at this stage.

ANSWERS

Sentence work
Verbs
1. teeth — hold
   hands — bite
   legs — see
   eyes — hear
   ears — run
2. The boy <u>cleans</u> his teeth.
   She <u>eats</u> an apple.
   They <u>talk</u> to the dentist.
   She <u>sits</u> in the chair.
   He <u>looks</u> at their teeth.

Questions and answers
How often do you clean your teeth?
When did you go to the dentist?
What is the name of your dentist?

Word work
ai and ay words
2. r<u>ai</u>n tr<u>ay</u> sn<u>ai</u>l
   spr<u>ay</u> tr<u>ai</u>n t<u>ai</u>l

Words with similar meanings
1. individual answers
2. individual answers

Homework suggestions
- Write a short piece of factual writing, using headings etc. about a topic of interest to the child, e.g. a pet.
- Give a number of nouns for children to find possible related verbs.
- Collect synonyms for a number of words selected by the group.

Year 2 Unit 16 Copymaster 1

Name _____ **Date** _____

Food I Like

My favourite meals

For breakfast I like to have _____
_____

My favourite lunch is _____
_____

In the evening I like to eat _____
_____

Types of food

```
┌─────────────────────────────────────────┐
│                                         │
│                                         │
│                                         │
│                                         │
└─────────────────────────────────────────┘
```

A diagram of my favourite foods.

My favourite vegetables are _____

The fruits I like best are _____

If I have meat, the type I like most is _____

My favourite puddings are _____

The drinks I most like are _____

Objective: To write an information page about food

On Target English © Hilary Frost 2001

a-e, ai and ay words

The answers to these clues are hidden in the box. Some words go across, some go down.
Colour the words you find, then write them next to the clues they answer.

r	u	n	w	a	y	f	s
a	p	a	l	e	z	n	t
i	s	i	x	h	a	y	r
l	p	l	a	t	e	t	a
w	r	s	n	a	i	l	y
a	a	r	a	i	n	m	g
y	y	w	a	l	a	n	e
o	d	d	t	r	a	y	g
p	l	a	y	t	i	m	e

1 aeroplanes land on this _____
2 trains, stations and track _____
3 hit with a hammer to hold wood together _____
4 antonym for 'early' _____
5 small garden creature that carries its shell on its back _____
6 drops of water falling from clouds _____
7 a small country road _____
8 a fine shower of water _____
9 a lost animal _____
10 for carrying cups and plates _____
11 the time for fun between lessons _____

Objective: To practise *a-e*, *ai* and *ay* words

Unit 17 Lofty the Giant

Curriculum references

England (Year 2 Term 3)
Range: Non-chronological reports
Objectives:

Text level work
5 to read about authors from information on book covers; to become aware of authorship and publication
12 to write simple evaluations of books read and discussed giving reasons

Sentence level work
2 the need for grammatical agreement, matching verbs to nouns/pronouns correctly
5 to write in clear sentences using capital letters and full stops accurately

Word level work
1 to secure phonemic spellings from previous five terms
7 to spell words with common suffixes
11 to practise handwriting in conjunction with the phonic and spelling patterns (being learnt)
12 to use the four basic handwriting joins:
- diagonal joins to letters with ascenders

Wales
Range – Pupils should be given opportunities to:
3 write in response to a variety of stimuli, including classroom activities and personal experience
Skills
2 ... learn about the different purposes and functions of written language
4 write independently on subjects that are of interest to them
5 identify the purpose for which they write
7 punctuate:
- recognise that punctuation is essential to help a reader understand what is written
- punctuate their writing, be consistent in their use of capital letters, full stops
8 spell:
- use their knowledge of sound–symbol relationships and phonological patterns
- recognise and use simple spelling patterns
- write common letter strings with familiar and common words
- spell commonly occurring simple words
9 develop their handwriting:
- build on their knowledge of letter formation to join letters in words

Language development – Pupils should be given opportunities to:
1 consider the vocabulary, grammar and structures of written standard English

Scotland (AT/PoS Level A/B)
Functional writing – Write briefly in an appropriate form for a variety of practical purposes.
Punctuation and structure – Use capital letters and full stops correctly.
Spelling – Spell frequently used words accurately through using a simple wordbank or dictionary. The learning of spelling rules should support this.
Handwriting – Form letters and space words legibly in linked script.
Knowledge about language – Understand and use the terms: capital, full stop, sentence.

Northern Ireland
Purpose – describe; inform and explain; report
Range – simple records of observations
Expected outcomes:
- spell recognisably a range of familiar and important words
- use basic punctuation conventions, including capital letters, full stops
- write correctly structured sentences

On Target English

Interactive Big Book
- Discuss the purposes and functions of a book cover, using several, with different styles, to demonstrate. Pick out the title, author and illustrator (if shown). Discuss why the picture and impact of the cover is important, encouraging the reader to want to open the pages and, in a shop, to buy a copy.
- The pictures depicting Lofty give an opportunity to give further exposure to verbs as action words. Make a list on the board of the verbs the children suggest; then follow up the work in the previous unit by inviting suggestions for possible synonyms for all of these words.

Comprehension and Writing Skills
Making a book
Discuss the key functions in making a book, from the author, illustrator, editor/publisher, printer to bookseller.
About Lofty
Read the back cover copy blurb (a term the children should become familiar with) to ascertain which of the given sentences are true.
I have read ...
The writing activity, requiring the children to think carefully about a book they have read or shared, is framed to ease their task. A copy of the frame is included as copymaster 1 from this unit for those who might otherwise find the task too challenging.

Unit 17

Characters in my book
Guide the children towards the key and most significant characteristics of the characters, listing and carefully considering words that might be used to describe them.

ANSWERS

Comprehension
Making a book
The author of the book is Edward Keeling.
The pictures were drawn by William James.
The publisher is Longman.
Edward Keeling has written two other 'Lofty the Giant' books.
About Lofty
Lofty set out to help the villagers.
Lofty helped to mend a wall.
Lofty put a chimney pot back on a roof.
The villagers had a party for Lofty.

Sentence and Word Skills
Using has and have
The same broad principles apply as in the earlier units when encouraging the children to ensure verb/noun (or pronoun) agreement, i.e. basic explanation plus lots of oral work.
Capital letters in titles
How and when to use capitals in titles often confuses children, especially as many books have the title on the front cover in block capitals throughout. The second part of the activity provides a chance to practise capital letters (and question marks) in the context of simple sentences.
ir, ur and er words
Although it need not confuse the children, er when it comes at the end of a word is called a 'schwa vowel', which is rather like a grunt, as in the short word 'a'. It is most frequently a schwa vowel sound, though it does have the same sound value as ur and ir when in the medial position of a word, such as 'herd'. Care is needed as ire (as in fire) normally represents a phoneme which is distinct and different from ir. Copymaster 2 from this unit will provide support and extra practice as required.
Adding ed
Here practised as a suffix, the task nevertheless provides an opportunity to secure the concept of verbs being modified to indicate tense.

ANSWERS

Sentence work
Using has and have
1 Lofty the Giant has no friends.
   The villagers have always been afraid of him.
   He has never hurt anyone.
   He has found ways to help them.
   Now the villagers have decided to have a party for Lofty.
2 individual answers
Capital letters in titles
1 Lofty the Giant Saves the Day
   Lofty the Giant Sorts Things Out
2 Have you read any Lofty the Giant books?
   Did James enjoy the Lofty story he read?
   Did Edward Keeling write the Lofty books?

Word work
ir, ur and er words
burn kerb nurse shirt
nerve skirt fern purse
Adding ed
1 licked jumped locked kicked packed washed rained
2 individual answers

Homework suggestions
- Use copymaster 1 from this unit to write a review of a book read at home.
- List and learn the spellings of an appropriate number of ir, ur and er words (say, three of each).

Year 2 Unit 17 Copymaster 1

Name _____ **Date** _____

I have read …

Title _____

Author _____

Artist _____

Publisher _____

This book is about _____

_____

_____

The main characters are _____

_____

The best thing about this book is _____

_____

_____

The worst thing about this book is _____

_____

_____

Objective: To write about a book you have read

On Target English © Hilary Frost 2001

Year 2 Unit 17 Copymaster 2

Name _____ Date _____

ir, *ur* and *er* words

Add the missing letters to each of these words:

b _ _ d   h _ _ d   b _ _ glar

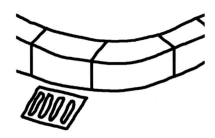  

k _ _ b   sh _ _ t   n _ _ se

h _ _ t   p _ _ ch   ch _ _ ch

Write a sentence for each of these words:
first _____
purse _____
fern _____
furniture _____

Objective: To practise *ir*, *ur* and *er* words

On Target English © Hilary Frost 2001

Unit 18 Who am I?

Curriculum references

England (Year 2 Term 3)
Range: Non-chronological reports
Objectives

Text level work
8 to discuss meanings of words and phrases that create humour ...
11 ... to invent own riddles, language puzzles etc.

Sentence level work
2 ... using simple gender forms correctly
6 to turn statements into questions, learning a range of 'wh' words typically used to open questions and to add question marks

Word level work
1 to secure phonemic spellings from previous five terms
6 to investigate words which have the same spelling patterns but different sounds
9 new words from particular topics, to build individual collections of personal interest or significant words
11 to practise handwriting in conjunction with the phonic and spelling patterns (being learnt)
12 to use the four basic handwriting joins:
• diagonal joins to letters with ascenders

Wales
Range – Pupils should be given opportunities to:
3 write in response to a variety of stimuli, including classroom activities and personal experience
4 write in a range of forms
7 make choices about vocabulary
Skills
1 write with confidence, fluency and accuracy
2 learn about the different purposes and functions of written language
7 punctuate:
• punctuate their writing, be consistent in their use of capital letters, full stops and question marks
8 spell:
• use their knowledge of sound–symbol relationships and phonological patterns
• recognise and use simple spelling patterns
• write common letter strings with familiar and common words
• spell commonly occurring simple words
9 develop their handwriting:
• build on their knowledge of letter formation to join letters in words
Language development – Pupils should be given opportunities to:
1 consider the vocabulary, grammar and structures of written standard English

3 develop their interest in words and their meanings, and extend their vocabulary through consideration ... of words with similar meanings

Scotland (AT/PoS Level A/B)
Personal writing – Write briefly and in an appropriate sequence about a personal experience, giving an indication of feelings, using adequate vocabulary.
Punctuation and structure – Use capital letters and full stops correctly.
Spelling – Spell frequently used words accurately through using a simple wordbank or dictionary.
Handwriting – Form letters and space words legibly in linked script.
Knowledge about language – Understand and use the terms: capital, full stop, sentence.

Northern Ireland
Purpose – Pupils should have the opportunity to write for a variety of purposes
Range – Pupils should have the opportunity to write for a variety of forms
Expected outcomes:
• spell recognisably a range of familiar and important words
• use basic punctuation conventions, including capital letters, full stops and question marks

On Target English

Interactive Big Book
• Share the riddles on the page, and then make up additional riddles from suggestions made by the children.
• Use the illustrations to collect gender-specific words. Add others when all the illustrated possibilities have been exhausted.
• A similar activity, collecting all the words which include 'ou' or 'ow' graphemes suggested by the illustrations, might be shared before the section in the Sentence and Word Skills book is introduced.

Comprehension and Writing Skills
People who help us
The cloze passage requires literal responses to the riddles.
How do they help us?
Full sentence answers are required, giving another opportunity to secure the structure and punctuation of sentences.
Guess who
The activity has been devised to ease children into writing riddles, but note, the point of the task is for the child to add another clue to each riddle once they have guessed who it is.

Making riddles
Using the same form encourage the children to think of other riddles they can write around a different topic. Copymaster 1 from this unit provides more support.

ANSWERS

Comprehension
People who help us
The postwoman and the milkman go to lots of houses and flats.
The bus driver and the policewoman wear uniforms.
The postwoman and the milkman sometimes get chased by dogs.
The postwoman delivers letters and the milkman delivers milk.

How do they help us?
The policewoman helps to keep people safe.
The postwoman brings our letters and postcards.
The bus driver stops at bus-stops to collect people and let them get off the bus.
The milkman goes to lots of houses and flats to deliver milk.

Sentence and Word Skills
Girl or boy, man or woman
Consider how some words relate only to males, some to females, while some nouns can be used for either gender. Invite the children to make suggestions, which can be listed appropriately on the board.
Develop by using the opportunity to share with the children words that can be used in place of nouns, i.e. pronouns. Demonstrate how repetitive and clumsy sentences would be if we didn't use such words. Invite the children to suggest such words, and list these on the board. Then sort the list into those for males, those used for females and those that can be used either for males or females.

Making questions
Discuss how questions can be constructed from statements, and vice versa, by rearranging the words and using the main question words. List on the board the 'wh' question words practised previously in Units 15 and 16, i.e. Who, Where, When, Why, Which, What.

ou and ow words
ow was taught in Unit 9 as the phoneme 'o', as in throw. In this unit the other main phoneme ow represents, i.e. as in cow, is taught with ou as in cloud. Copymaster 2 from this unit provides extra practice.

Collecting words
The main purpose of this simple task is to encourage the pupils to take responsibility for collecting their own words in lists or spelling logs and/or for creating a class dictionary. Some children might be given other useful topics on which to base word collections.

ANSWERS

Sentence work
Girl or boy, man or woman?
1 king bride boy policeman policewoman girl bridegroom queen
2 individual answers

Making questions
Examples could include:
1 Who puts the milk on the doorstep?
   What is on the policewoman's car?
2 individual answers

Word work
ou and ow words
A cow gives us milk.
A queen wears a crown.
A round shape is called a circle.
Brown is the colour of soil.
Rain falls from clouds.

Collecting words
individual answers

Homework suggestions
- Make up some riddles about members of the family.
- Write two questions that you think your pet might ask you if it could speak.
- Collect, and learn to spell, an appropriate number of ou and ow words.

Year 2 Unit 18 Copymaster 1

Name _____ Date _____

Riddles

Write a short riddle clue to go with each picture.

1

_____
_____
_____

2

_____
_____
_____

3

_____
_____
_____

4

_____
_____
_____

Objective: To write riddles

ou and ow words

Sort the words into four rhyme families.

> drown pound growl sprout frown
> shout round sound owl howl
> down clown found scout about prowl

____ ____ ____ ____
____ ____ ____ ____
____ ____ ____ ____
____ ____ ____ ____

Fill in the missing *ou* or *ow* words in the pictures.

Objective: To spell words with *ou* and *ow*

Unit 19 Moving People

Curriculum references

England (Year 2 Term 3)
Range: Non-chronological reports
Objectives:

> **Text level work**
> 14 to pose questions and record these in writing, prior to reading non-fiction to find answers
> 21 to write non-chronological reports based on structure of known texts

> **Sentence level work**
> 3 to use standard form of verbs in speaking and writing
> 4 to use commas in lists
> 5 to write in clear sentences using capital letters and full stops accurately

> **Word level work**
> 1 to secure phonemic spellings from previous five terms
> 11 to practise handwriting in conjunction with the phonic and spelling patterns (being learnt)
> 12 to use the four basic handwriting joins:
> • diagonal joins to letters with ascenders

Wales
Range – Pupils should be given opportunities to:
3 write in response to a variety of stimuli, including classroom activities and personal experience
4 write in a range of forms, incorporating some of the characteristics of those forms
Skills
1 write with confidence, fluency and accuracy
2 ... learn about the different purposes and functions of written language
4 write independently on subjects that are of interest to them
7 punctuate:
• recognise that punctuation is essential to help a reader understand what is written
• punctuate their writing, be consistent in their use of capital letters, full stops and question marks, and begin to use commas
8 spell:
• recognise and use simple spelling patterns
• write common letter strings with familiar and common words
• spell words with common prefixes
9 develop their handwriting:
• build on their knowledge of letter formation to join letters in words
Language development – Pupils should be given opportunities to:
3 develop their interest in words and their meanings, and extend their vocabulary through consideration ... of opposites

Scotland (AT/PoS Level A/B)
Functional writing – Write briefly in an appropriate form for a variety of practical purposes.
Punctuation and structure – Use capital letters and full stops correctly.
Spelling – Spell frequently used words accurately through using a simple wordbank or dictionary.
Handwriting – Form letters and space words legibly in linked script.
Knowledge about language – Understand and use the terms capital, full stop, sentence.

Northern Ireland
Purpose – inform and explain; record findings
Range – simple records of observations; descriptions of people or places
Expected outcomes:
- spell recognisably a range of familiar and important words
- use basic punctuation conventions, including capital letters, full stops and question marks
- write correctly structured sentences

On Target English

Interactive Big Book
- Ask children to consider the different types of transport illustrated. Discuss the different circumstances for which each type of transport is appropriate.
- Look at the matrix on page 41 together, or copy this onto the board. Encourage children to sort the transport pictures into the three categories

Comprehension and Writing Skills
Travelling
The activity requires literal responses to the passage and the completion of sentences accordingly.
Ways to travel
If the class or group work has been undertaken as suggested above, the children might be encouraged to work independently to complete the matrix. For those for whom the actual drawing of the matrix could be a barrier, a frame on copymaster 1 from this unit is provided.
How animals move
Again, a copy of the frame (copymaster 1 from this unit) might help some children complete this activity.
Using the chart
Encourage those that are able to use the matrix in the wider context of presenting information about how animals move, which should include headings and sub-headings, short, direct sentences and possibly diagrams or pictures. For this to work effectively, considerable teacher discussion and support will be needed.

Unit 19

ANSWERS

Comprehension
Travelling
The way we travel depends on how far we need to go and how quickly we need to get there.
If we were going a long way in this country we would go on a bus, coach, train, car or motorbike.
We need to be older before we can drive a car.
We travel on a ship or an aeroplane if we are going to another country.

Ways to travel

Land	Air	Water
car	aeroplane	boat
train	balloon	tanker
bus	helicopter	submarine

Sentence and Word Skills

Verbs – present and past
This section brings together the earlier work on tenses, highlighting the use of the suffixes ing and ed, but also revising examples of irregular forms. Spend some time ensuring the terms 'present' and 'past' are clearly understood.

Using commas and full stops
Commas in lists have been practised previously, but in this unit the two last items in the lists are deliberately separated by 'or' rather than 'and'.

Words ending in ss, ff, ll
These are the most frequently occurring double letters at the ends of words, and as they feature in many of the words early writers might use, then time spent teaching the related spelling patterns is worth the effort. Copymaster 2 from this unit provides support.

Prefixes
In Unit 14 we introduced the notion of how a prefix (un-) could modify a root word, forming its antonym. There are other prefixes that act in the same way, one of the most common of which is dis-, which is the subject of this activity.

ANSWERS

Sentence work
Verbs – present and past
1   present   past
    jumping   asked
    watching   finished
    finishing   talked
    asking   watched
    talking   jumped
2   meeting   met   flying   flew   sinking   sank
    running   ran   going   went   driving   drove

Using commas and full stops
1   If you want to visit Manchester you can go by bus, coach, taxi, train, car or bike.

Gran says she will never go in a helicopter, airliner, submarine, balloon or spacecraft.
2   individual answers

Word work
Words ending in ss, ff, ll
cross   puff   call
cliff   miss   yell
sniff   mess   fall
kiss   doll   dress

Prefixes
1   disappear   disagree
    distrust   disobey
2   individual answers

Homework suggestions
- Make two lists of verbs: those that have ed added to make the past tense, and those that are changed in another way.
- Learn to spell an appropriate number of words with the prefixes dis or un.

Year 2 Unit 19 Copymaster 1

Name _____ **Date** _____

Sorting Information

This chart is about _____

The chart has shown that _____

_____

Objective: To convey information in a chart form

On Target English © Hilary Frost 2001

ss, ff, ll endings

Sort the words in the box into six rhyme families.

smell	stiff	dress	spell	less	grill	spill	cross
fluff	cliff	sniff	stuff	drill	gruff	fell	puff
still	gloss	biff	press	moss	yell	mess	boss

___ ___ ___ ___ ___ ___ ___ ___
___ ___ ___ ___ ___ ___ ___ ___
___ ___ ___ ___ ___ ___ ___ ___
___ ___ ___ ___ ___ ___ ___ ___

Write a verb to say what each of these people is doing.
(Each word ends in *ing*.)

Objective: To spell words with *ss*, *ff* and *ll*

Unit 20 Days of the Week

Curriculum references

England (Year 2 Term 3)
Range: Texts with language play
Objectives:

> **Text level work**
> 8 to discuss meanings of words and phrases that create humour, and sound effects in poetry
> 11 to use humorous verse as a structure for children to write their own by adaptation, mimicry or substitution

> **Sentence level work**
> 3 to use standard form of verbs in speaking and writing
> 5 to write in clear sentences using capital letters and full stops accurately

> **Word level work**
> 1 to secure phonemic spellings from previous five terms
> 11 to practise handwriting in conjunction with the phonic and spelling patterns (being learnt)
> 12 to use the four basic handwriting joins:
> • diagonal joins to letters with ascenders

Wales
Range – Pupils should be given opportunities to:
3 write in response to a variety of stimuli, including poems
4 write in a range of forms, incorporating some of the characteristics of those forms; the range should include poems
7 make choices about vocabulary and organise imaginative and factual writing in different ways, e.g. a cumulative pattern in a poem
Skills
2 learn about the different purposes and functions of written language
3 recognise the alphabetic nature of writing and discriminate between letters
7 punctuate:
• punctuate their writing, be consistent in their use of capital letters
8 spell:
• write each letter of the alphabet
• use their knowledge of sound–symbol relationships and phonological patterns
9 develop their handwriting:
• build on their knowledge of letter formation to join letters in words
Language development – Pupils should be given opportunities to:
3 develop their interest in words and their meanings … opposites

Scotland (AT/PoS Level A/B)
Imaginative writing – Write a brief imaginative poem, with discernible organisation and using adequate vocabulary.
Punctuation and structure – Use capital letters correctly.
Handwriting – Form letters and space words legibly in linked script.
Knowledge about language – Understand and use the terms: letter, word, capital.

Northern Ireland
Purpose – express thoughts and feelings; develop their imagination
Range – poems
Expected outcomes:
• make use of names and order of the letters of the alphabet
• use basic punctuation conventions, including capital letters

On Target English

Interactive Big Book
• Share the poem with the children. Notice the rhyme pattern, and discuss the overall (repeating) structure. Write on the board the days of the week and ask volunteers to suggest whether there are special events that recur regularly each week for them, as they do for the narrator of the poem.
• Share ideas for a final verse, though avoid writing it out as this forms part of the pupils' activities that follow.

Comprehension and Writing Skills
Which day?
The first comprehension activity requires a simple literal response (true/false) to the poem.
What happens?
These are questions requiring simple deduction. Use the opportunity to ensure that the children are writing in correctly structured and punctuated sentences.
Saturday
Before asking the children to try to create their own verse for Saturday, in a class or group session try to mimic the poem's style and pattern by writing some verses for what happens in school on each day of the week. Begin by noting some subjects for each verse and then collect some rhyming words. Notice that some lines can be contrived (e.g. 'change-your-vest day' and 'run-along day'). For this and the following task the frame in copymaster 1 from this unit will provide some support, where appropriate.
A Sunday verse
Allow/encourage some children to have a go on their own with a final verse.

Teacher's Resource Book 2

Unit 20

ANSWERS

Comprehension
Which day?
1 true
2 false
3 true
4 true
5 false
6 true

What happens?
individual answers

Sentence and Word Skills
Naming word or action word?
Another opportunity to embed the terms and concepts of noun and verb.

More proper nouns
Previously the main emphasis on proper nouns had been on names of people and places, so this unit gives more attention to the proper nouns that are associated with the calendar. Copymaster 2 from this unit provides extra practice.

Vowels and consonants
These two terms become increasingly significant, and this unit introduces the five vowels as being the 'key' sounds that must appear in every word in English. However, in a few situations the letter 'y' acts in place of 'i' as a vowel (e.g. by, try)

Opposites
Another opportunity to secure the notion of antonyms. As an extension, remind the children of words which can be turned into their antonym by the simple addition of a prefix (e.g. un, dis).

ANSWERS

Sentence work
Naming word or action word?
We <u>run</u> after the <u>football</u>.
I <u>like</u> <u>swimming</u> in the <u>pool</u>.
Gran <u>eats</u> a sticky <u>bun</u>.

More proper nouns
1 The five days in the week that we go to school are Monday, Tuesday, Wednesday, Thursday and Friday.
2 Monday September May Wednesday Sunday February

Word work
Vowels and consonants
1 <u>o</u>ne tw<u>o</u> thr<u>ee</u> f<u>ou</u>r f<u>i</u>v<u>e</u> s<u>i</u>x s<u>e</u>v<u>e</u>n <u>eig</u>ht n<u>i</u>n<u>e</u> t<u>e</u>n
2 <u>e</u>l<u>e</u>v<u>e</u>n tw<u>e</u>lv<u>e</u> th<u>i</u>rt<u>ee</u>n f<u>ou</u>rt<u>ee</u>n f<u>i</u>ft<u>ee</u>n s<u>i</u>xt<u>ee</u>n s<u>e</u>v<u>e</u>nt<u>ee</u>n <u>eig</u>ht<u>ee</u>n n<u>i</u>n<u>e</u>t<u>ee</u>n tw<u>e</u>nty

Opposites
1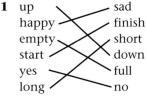
up — no
happy — sad
empty — full
start — finish
yes — no
long — short

(lines connect: up–down; happy–sad; empty–full; start–finish; yes–no; long–short)

2 carry on – stop; stay in – go out; end of school – beginning of school

Homework suggestions
- Learn a verse of the poem by heart.
- Write four verbs for actions done at home, and four nouns that name things at home.
- Write the days of the week, and underline all the vowel letters in the seven words.

105

Year 2 Unit 20 Copymaster 1

Name _____ **Date** _____

My Own Poem

Saturday's a

_____ *day,*

_____ *day,*

_____ *day,*

_____ *day,*

When work is done.

Sunday's a

_____ *day,*

_____ *day,*

_____ *day,*

_____ *day,*

_____

Objective: To write a poem

On Target English © Hilary Frost 2001

Proper Nouns

Underline the proper nouns in these sentences:

Tom and Alice ran to school. It was Monday 12th of May and their class at Shelley Primary School was going to London for the day. They were feeling very excited.

Mr Desai, their teacher, had arranged for a trip to the Tower of London and St Paul's Cathedral. Afterwards they were going to have lunch in Green Park and then see Buckingham Palace. Mrs James and Mrs Nicholson were going too, to help Mr Desai look after the class.

Tom and Alice had been to Cambridge with Aunty Sue and Uncle Mike, but they had never been to London before.

Objective: To identify proper nouns

Name _____ **Date** _____

Term 3 Assessment of Progress: Comprehension

When I Was One

When I was One,
I had just begun.
When I was Two,
I was nearly new.
When I was Three,
I was hardly me.
When I was Four,
I was not much more.
When I was Five,
I was just alive.
But now I am Six,
I'm as clever as clever.
So I think I'll be Six now
for ever and ever.

A. A. Milne

Teacher's Note for spelling assessment on page 4
First, discuss the large picture and the pictures around it, ensuring the children know what each picture represents. Ask the children to write the name of each small picture in the box underneath it.
Read through the passage from the full text below while the children just listen. Give the children the first word and ask them to write it in the first space. Check that each child has understood what to do and has written the word in the first space. Continue reading the passage for the second time, stopping at each missing word to allow time for the word to be written by the children in a space on their page. Repeat the words as necessary.

My <u>party</u> was fun. I had some <u>good</u> presents.
The <u>thing</u> I liked best <u>was</u> my <u>new</u> bike.
Gran gave me a <u>football</u>.
Mum and Dad <u>said</u> we could go to the <u>park</u> to <u>play</u> with it <u>when</u> the rain stopped.

Name _____ **Date** _____

These questions are about the poem *When I Was One* and the picture.

Fill in the missing words:

1 Winston has _____ friends at his party.
2 Mum is carrying in the _____ .
3 There are _____ candles on it.
4 He hasn't opened his _____ yet.
5 He has _____ presents.
6 The puppy is asleep on the _____ .
7 One of his presents is a _____ .

Tick the right box:

8 He was 'hardly me' when he was:
  one ☐   two ☐   three ☐   four ☐   five ☐

9 He was 'just alive' when he was:
  one ☐   two ☐   three ☐   four ☐   five ☐

10 He was 'nearly new' when he was:
  one ☐   two ☐   three ☐   four ☐   five ☐

Write a sentence to answer these questions.

11 What does the poet mean by 'When I was Two, I was nearly new'?
_____

12 Did you enjoy this poem? What are your reasons?
_____
_____

On Target English © Hilary Frost 2001

Name _____ **Date** _____

Term 3 Assessment of Progress: Writing

Birthdays

Write a list of the things you like most about birthdays.
_____
_____
_____
_____

What are the things you don't like about birthdays?
_____
_____
_____

Write about what happened at your last birthday.
_____
_____
_____
_____
_____
_____

Term 3 Assessment of Progress: Spelling

   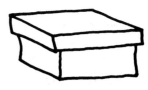

My _____ was fun. I had some _____ presents.

The _____ I liked best _____ my

_____ bike.

Gran gave me a _____.

Mum and Dad _____ we could go to the _____

to _____ with it _____ the rain stopped.

Appendix 1: Spelling Specials

The following lists of words are recommended for look, say, cover, write, check strategies, but are arranged so as to focus, in most cases, on particular and significant common spelling features.

They cover all the high-frequency words listed in the NLS Framework for Teaching (List 1), together with a few other significant high-frequency words that children use. In addition, it should be noted that the children should by this stage be confident in spelling months of the year and numbers to twenty, as well as their own name and address and the school's name and address.

In some cases the Unit content and the word lists have common spelling features, but the main purpose of these photocopiable cut-out lists is to ensure that all the most important words are covered during the year. To this end it is recommended that the 'Spelling Specials' are used for homework, combined with a regular weekly spelling test.

These words will be returned to in Y3 for further consolidation, but if most of the children can master most of these spellings in Y2 they will have a sound foundation on which to build their spelling competence.

OTE2 Spelling Special Unit 1	OTE2 Spelling Special Unit 2	OTE2 Spelling Special Unit 3	OTE2 Spelling Special Unit 4
but	old	good	our
did	two	took	out
dig	too	look	about
had	off	school	
bed	jump		how
got	will	put	now
ran	red	push	down
		blue	
OTE2 Spelling Special Unit 5	**OTE2 Spelling Special Unit 6**	**OTE2 Spelling Special Unit 7**	**OTE2 Spelling Special Unit 8**
love	what	time	came
more	when	back	made
one	where	from	make
some	who		name
		was	take
live	were	want	
have		water	

OTE2 Spelling Special Unit 9	OTE2 Spelling Special Unit 10	OTE2 Spelling Special Unit 11	OTE2 Spelling Special Unit 12
may	many	could	Sunday
way	much	should	Monday
away	once	would	Tuesday
play	with		Wednesday
	not	can't	Thursday
again	has	don't	Friday
said			Saturday

OTE2 Spelling Special Unit 13	OTE2 Spelling Special Unit 14	OTE2 Spelling Special Unit 15	OTE2 Spelling Special Unit 16
half	after	just	tree
help	next	last	been
here	over	must	seen
home	very	first	three
house	your		green

OTE2 Spelling Special Unit 17	OTE2 Spelling Special Unit 18	OTE2 Spelling Special Unit 19	OTE2 Spelling Special Unit 20
than	boy	all	night
that	girl	ball	because
there	brother	call	little
their	sister		people
them	man	his	another
then		him	laugh
these		her	door

Year 2 Handwriting Copymaster 1

Name _____ **Date** _____

Trace and copy the patterns and words.

an

an   an   an   an   an   an

van   man   pan   ran   can   fan

en

en   en   en   en   en   en

den   hen   men   pen   ten   Ben

ar

ar   ar   ar   ar   ar   ar

bar   car   far   jar   tar

in

in   in   in   in   in   in

bin   din   tin   win   fin

Objective: To practise diagonal joins to letters without ascenders

On Target English © Hilary Frost 2000

Year 2 Handwriting Copymaster 2

Name _____ **Date** _____

Trace and copy the patterns and words.

an an an en en en ar ar ar in in in

and hand band sand land

went sent bent tent lent

bar bark barn art cart dart

bin bind fin find win wind

Objective: To practise diagonal joins to letters without ascenders

On Target English © Hilary Frost 2000

Year 2 Handwriting Copymaster 3

Name _____ **Date** _____

Trace and copy the patterns and words.

am

am am am am am am

ham dam jam ram yam

ap

ap ap ap ap ap ap

tap bap map lap cap nap

is

is is is is is is

his fist list mist hiss miss

ea

ea ea ea ea ea ea

pea sea tea flea meat beat

Objective: To practise diagonal joins to letters without ascenders

On Target English © Hilary Frost 2000

Year 2 Handwriting Copymaster 4

Name _____ **Date** _____

Trace and copy the patterns and words.

am am am   as as as   is is is   ea ea ea

ramp   camp   lamp   damp

toast   past   fast   mast

hiss   kiss   miss   bliss   list   mist

team   steam   stream   cream   scream

Objective: To practise diagonal joins to letters without ascenders

On Target English © Hilary Frost 2000

Name _____ **Date** _____

Trace and copy the patterns and words.

on

on on on on on on

pond fond long song moon spoon

oa

oa oa oa oa oa oa

road toad load cool fool goal

ow

ow ow ow ow ow ow

bow cow how now row sow

or

or or or or or or

born horn torn port sport short

Objective: To practise horizontal joins to letters without ascenders

Year 2 Handwriting Copymaster 6

Name _____ **Date** _____

Trace and copy the patterns and words.

on on on oa oa oa ow ow ow or or or

bone bone cone stone throne scone

boast coast roast toast

owl howl growl

brown crown frown

bore store core score wore swore

Objective: To practise horizontal joins to letters without ascenders

On Target English © Hilary Frost 2000

Year 2 Handwriting Copymaster 7

Name _____ **Date** _____

Trace and copy the patterns and words.

wi

wi   wi   wi   wi   wi   wi

writ   with   wig   win   wind

we

we   we   we   we   we   we

web   wed   well   were   west

wa

wa   wa   wa   wa   wa   wa

wax   way   was   wash   wasp

wo

wo   wo   wo   wo   wo   wo

won   wood   work   wool   worm

Objective: To practise horizontal joins to letters without ascenders

On Target English © Hilary Frost 2000

Year 2 Handwriting Copymaster 8

Name _____ **Date** _____

Trace and copy the patterns and words.

wi wi wi we we we wa wa wa wo wo wo wo

win wind window win wring swing

went week weed weep sweet

was wagon walk wall wash

woman wonder woodpecker

workman world

Objective: To practise horizontal joins to letters without ascenders

On Target English © Hilary Frost 2000

Name _____ **Date** _____

Trace and copy the patterns and words.

at

at   at   at   at   at   at

bat   cat   fat   hat   mat   rat

et

et   et   et   et   et   et

bet   vet   set   let   met   net

it

it   it   it   it   it   it

bit   fit   hit   lit   mit   sit

Objective: To practise horizontal joins to letters without ascenders

Year 2 Handwriting Copymaster 10

Name _____ **Date** _____

Trace and copy the patterns and words.

at at at et et et it it it

that   what   water

father   path   bath

bet   better   wet   wetter   wettest

itch   ditch   pitch

stitch   switch

Objective: To practise horizontal joins to letters without ascenders

Name _____ **Date** _____

Trace and copy the patterns and words.

al

al   al   al   al   al   al

ball   tall   hall   fall   call

cl

cl   cl   cl   cl   cl   cl

clap   clip   clock   click

il

il   il   il   il   il   il

mill   will   pill   fill   bill

Objective: To practise horizontal joins to letters without ascenders

Year 2 Handwriting Copymaster 12

Name _____ **Date** _____

Trace and copy the patterns and words.

al al al cl cl cl il il il

also   always   already

almost   altogether

class   day   clean

clever   clown   clue

drill frill grill spill skill still

Objective: To practise horizontal joins to letters without ascenders

On Target English © Hilary Frost 2000

Year 2 Handwriting Copymaster 13

Name _____ **Date** _____

Trace and copy the letter patterns.

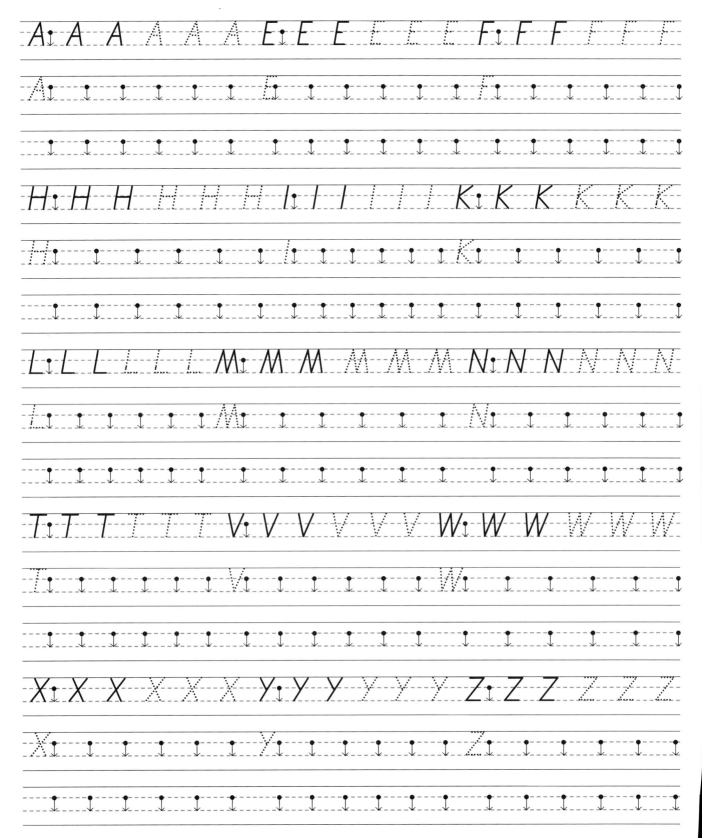

Objective: To practise writing capitals without curves

On Target English © Hilary Frost 2000

Year 2 Handwriting Copymaster 14

Name _____ **Date** _____

Trace and copy the letter patterns.

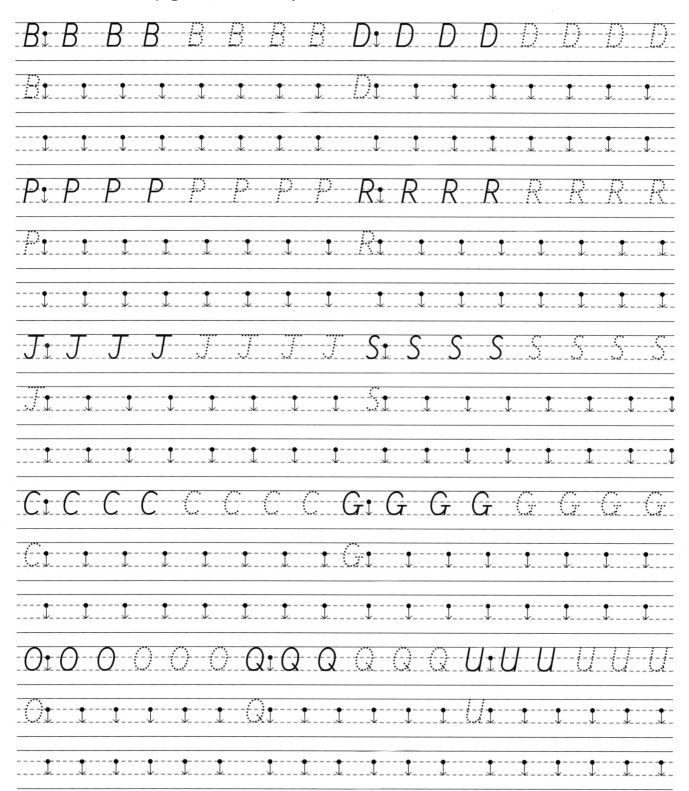

Objective: To practise writing capitals with curves

On Target English © Hilary Frost 2000

Year 2 Handwriting Copymaster 15

Name _____ **Date** _____

On Target English © Hilary Frost 2000